Also by Leo V. Kanawada Jr.

Non-fiction

*Franklin D. Roosevelt's Diplomacy
and American Catholics, Italians, and Jews*

*Something Worthwhile:
The Life and Times of The Parkway Community Church:
1628-1981*

*Captain, Infantry:
A Vietnam War Memoir*

*The Jubilee Jamboree:
A Personal Boy Scouting Memoir*

Novelized History

The Holocaust Diaries

Book One: *Souls of the Just*

Book Two: *The Righteous and the Just*

Book Three: *A Homeland for the Just*

Book Four: *Saviors of the Just*

Book Five: *The Innocence of the Just*

Poetry

Some Thoughts Worthwhile:

A Short Book of Inspirational Poetry

Nascent Hues:

A Collection of my Original Poems: 1970-2014

Songbook

The First Ten:

Album of my Original Piano Compositions: 1968-2016

Thesis and Dissertation

George Clinton: First Governor of the State of New York
and American Independence

The Ethnic Factor in American Diplomacy
during the Presidency of Franklin D. Roosevelt: 1933-1939

GEORGE CLINTON

*An American Founding Father
and American Independence*

Leo V. Kanawada Jr.

authorHOUSE

AuthorHouse™
1663 Liberty Drive
Bloomington, IN 47403
www.authorhouse.com
Phone: 833-262-8899

Published by AuthorHouse 07/26/2022

ISBN: 978-1-6655-6475-5 (sc)
ISBN: 978-1-6655-6477-9 (hc)
ISBN: 978-1-6655-6478-6 (e)

Library of Congress Control Number: 2022913253

Print information available on the last page.

For my wife, Carol

my daughter, Kristina, and my son, Sean

and my cherished and precious grandchildren,

Alexandria, Kailee, Sean, Jr.,

Lily and Scott

Thomas Jefferson

Our Sacred Honor

"When in the course of human events, it becomes necessary for one people to dissolve the political bands which have connected them with another . . . a decent respect to the opinions of mankind requires that they should declare the causes which impel them to the separation.

We hold these truths to be self-evident: That all men are created equal, that they are endowed by their Creator with certain unalienable rights, that among these are life, liberty, and the pursuit of happiness . . .

The history of the present King of Great Britain is a history of repeated injuries . . . (He) is unfit to be the ruler of a free people . . .

We, therefore, the representatives of the United States of America, . . . appealing to the Supreme Judge of the world . . . do, in the name . . . of the good people of these colonies, solemnly publish and declare, That these United Colonies are, and of right ought to be, FREE AND INDEPENDENT STATES, . . . And, for the support of this declaration, with a firm reliance on the protection of Divine Providence, we mutually pledge to each other our lives, our fortunes, and our sacred honor."

Excerpted from the *Declaration of Independence*, July 4, 1776

Contents

Preface

George Clinton's early political career and his actions at the outbreak of the American Revolution provide evidence for an interesting case study of a New York leader and the decision for American independence. Most New Yorkers -- even most New York patriot leaders -- emphatically opposed independence as late as July of 1776. From all indications, the facts seem to reveal that Clinton himself hedged and vacillated on the question of independence. This much is certain: Clinton did not openly advocate independence, either in the Continental Congress or in New York, prior to the Declaration of Independence; he had no systematic "democratic" program worked out for his colony; and even prior to his election as governor of New York, he advocated no revolutionary changes for New York.

To say that Clinton was a radical and that his decision regarding independence sprang from an impulse for democratic reform in New York, is misleading. Rather, the key to understanding the emergence of Clinton rests with contingent political circumstances in New

York and Clinton's popularity as a military commander. Prior to the winter of 1775, Clinton was a firm supporter of the Livingston faction and followed a moderate course in regard to resistance to Parliament, but once Clinton became a general in the field of battle and devoted himself to the defense of New York, he won widespread fame and popularity. Only after other Americans had committed the colonies to independence did Clinton openly espouse separation, and that, together with his military fame, carried him into the office of governor.

CHAPTER ONE

Early Years

Charles Clinton, George Clinton's father, Scotch-Irish and a descendent of the Earls of Lincoln, was born in the county of Longford, Ireland, in 1690. Like many thousands of Scotch-Irish Presbyterians in Ireland at the time, the Clintons found life there intolerable. On May 20, 1729, Charles Clinton and seventy relatives and friends chartered the ship *George and Anne* and set sail for Philadelphia. After a tragic voyage, plagued by death and near mutiny, the settlers arrived at Cape Cod instead of Philadelphia. There they remained until the spring of 1731, when they departed for Ulster County, New York. After clearing a section of the wilderness not far from the west bank of the Hudson River, the small colony of settlers established their frontier community of Little Britain. At Little Britain, therefore, the American branch of a family was founded that was to give New York a great political dynasty.

Charles Clinton, open, generous and hospitable, an honest man and a loyal subject, was tall and of commanding appearance, endowed with a knowledge of literature and the arts, and known for his ability at mathematics. Although having won the favor of Governor George Clinton, who described him as a "good sort of a man," he declined the governor's favor of the office of sheriff of the City and County of New York or "any other commission." For a time, Charles Clinton preferred to enjoy and profit from his good meadow land, but after serving in the French and Indian War and as justice of the peace, he completed his public service as first judge of the Ulster Court of Common Pleas.

Born in an unpretentious, story-and-a-half cottage twenty feet square, situated on a narrow, long strip of land in the rolling hills of the Hudson Valley, George Clinton grew to manhood in a rural environment. Due to the fact that the province contained no public schools, Clinton's early education was entrusted to a young Scotch clergyman named Daniel Thain, a graduate of the University of Aberdeen. Young Clinton seems to have developed no strong enthusiasm for institutional religion, yet he did show a proper interest in the Presbyterian Church. It is significant to note at that time the influence of Anglicanism, so dominant in the southern counties, was practically non-existent in this part of New York. Very few Anglicans inhabited the Hudson River Valley before the Revolution, and those few were widely scattered and ministered to by a single missionary in Newburgh.

Clinton, like other young boys, experienced the rigors of colonial life in Ulster County, but found himself more disposed to the military. At the age of eighteen, he boarded the privateer, *Defiance*, at New York harbor, and during the ensuing year, he suffered much hardship and distress. Returning to New York on August 14, 1758, with a meager share of the prize money, George Clinton possibly began to serve with his father and brother, James, in the campaign against Fort Frontenac, present day Kingston, New York. In the fall of 1759, Clinton obtained the appointed position of clerk of Ulster County by the governor. Although he became acquainted with law, he grew restless again, and in the spring of 1760, George Clinton was commissioned a lieutenant in his brother's regiment. Clinton's only experience as a soldier before the outbreak of the Revolution was with the British force that captured Montreal in 1760.

George Clinton returned home and was appointed clerk of the Ulster County Court of Common Pleas, and soon went to New York City to study law in the office of William Smith. Smith, an eminent lawyer educated at Yale, in conjunction with William Livingston and John Morin Scott, constantly plagued the royal government of the province with tongue and pen. From this point until the outbreak of the Revolution, Clinton developed a close friendship not only with William Smith, but also with other members of the Livingston faction.

After three years of vigorous study, Clinton was commissioned attorney-at-law on September 12, 1764, by Governor Cadwallader

Colden and admitted to practice in the Mayor's Court of Common Pleas in the province. Clinton's busy schedule did allow him to continue as a surveyor of Ulster County and the New York-New Jersey boundary. Inasmuch as the twenty-six, year-old rural lawyer enjoyed his father's profession, he still distinguished himself as a lawyer and gained sufficient confidence from the people to become appointed surrogate of Ulster County on August 26, 1765.

Clinton's years as a law student in New York City exposed him to the colony's grievances toward imperial Britain as well as to the intricacies of New York politics. During this period of colonial protest, Clinton aligned himself with the Livingston faction and was elected to the New York General Assembly. An analysis, therefore, of provincial politics will go a long way in ascertaining the reasons for George Clinton's attachment to the Livingston faction and for his election as a delegate to the General Assembly from Ulster County.

CHAPTER TWO

Delegate from Ulster County

During the 1760s, Clinton's actions and career were a result of the political, social, and economic conditions that prevailed in the county of Ulster and in the colony of New York. In order to ascertain Clinton's initial and continuing allegiance to the minority Livingston faction in New York politics and his election to the General Assembly in 1768, the tenor of the times in the province of New York must be revealed in its proper perspective.

The British imperial administrative system -- as it touched the colony of New York -- was flexible in character. The colony was not incorporated as an organic part of the English body politic. It was expected to provide funds for its own local public affairs, and, to a great extent with this object in view, large powers of self-government were granted to it. Like other colonies in the Empire, New York developed a vigorous political life of its own; the popular branch of the local legislature (the General Assembly), through its control of the purse, became the most important governmental power.

Prior to 1765, the governors and the Assembly were continuously engaged in conflict. The royal governor, representing the crown, received appointments directly from the king, whereas the Assembly, previously forced upon the proprietor, represented the inhabitants of the colony. The General Assembly refused to allow the governor's council to amend money bills or appropriations, attempted to secure more frequent elections, and, throughout the colonial period, pressed for control over the judiciary. The governor, in turn, was primarily concerned with controlling the colony for the benefit of the imperial governmental interests in England. In the foreground of the American Revolution then, the call was sounded to mark the beginning of the contest for home rule and who should rule at home.

In New York, no political parties existed in fact, however, various centers of influence, counteracting each other, provided a stimulus in the contest for home rule. Basically, those under executive influence and attached to the governor's interest by special favors and the men who made use of the Assembly to thwart that interest was a division that remained somewhat permanent. Similarly, social and economic interests determined the nature of party alignment as it became manifested in the 1760s and 1770s. Of the three classes socially and economically distinguishable in the colony the most important was the small, closely related families of wealth, holding special privileges and grants of land, through whose influence the governor hoped to maintain secure control of the colony. These few families controlled a large part of the most valuable land in the province, ranging from Suffolk County on Long Island to the manorial estates of Livingston and Van Rensselaer on the Hudson to Albany.

A second class was composed of freemen and freehold electors, who purchased the right from the wealthy aristocrats to carry on an occupation either as a retailer, wholesaler, or independent handcrafts man. However, this class of freemen, by 1790, made up only twelve percent of the population of the colony and usually, in the political arena, supported the landed gentry.

Finally, the unfranchised made up the third class. These were the people whose estates were valued at less than forty pounds, or who were leasehold tenants, laboring for others, and those commonly called the "mechanics", the "inhabitants", or the shiftless, characterless class that inhabited New York City during the colonial period. Containing a majority of the male population of the colony over twenty-one years of age, this class was essentially without political privilege. As a result of these political and social conditions, the aristocracy was able to a great extent to control provincial politics. However, when the governor's influence diminished, and as the aristocracy became more secure in its titles and holdings, leaders of the aristocracy increasingly began to identify themselves with the Assembly.

Yet in the Assembly the political situation centered around rival factions -- the de Lanceyites and the Livingstons. The de Lanceyite and the Livingston factions were not exclusively based on class, for as we will see, the classes were divided and both factions found it necessary to court the lower classes in order to maintain their influence in New York politics.

During the eighteenth century, the de Lancey family of New York City, under the leadership of James de Lancey, won control of the colonial Assembly. The de Lanceyites, composed mainly of large property-owners -- landowners, merchants of wealth and political influence -- were essentially conservatives, and would support the crown if their trade would be secure.

The real leadership, however, of the de Lanceyite faction, in the period from 1765 until the Revolution, derived from Oliver de Lancey. Oliver, a wealthy merchant of New York City, courted the radical Sons of Liberty and by doing so, maintained the de Lanceyite supremacy in the Assembly to the discomfort of the Livingstons. William Smith, the eminent Presbyterian lawyer, critical of British policy and vigorously opposed to the influence of Anglicanism, complained that the de Lanceys "dupe the people to gain ascendency in the Assembly [in order to] rule govr's, sway the ministry, and inslave the colony."

Although the de Lanceyites dominated the Assembly, their political supremacy was strongly contested by a group led by great landed proprietors and able lawyers. This group, the Livingston faction, led by William Livingston, William Smith, and John Morin Scott, attracted those who wished to curb the king's prerogative, end corruption and favoritism in government, and restrain the power of the Anglican Church. The dissenting congregations –- Methodists, Presbyterians, Dutch Reformed, and German Reformed -- resented the fact that they were taxed to support the Episcopal establishment and feared the Anglican attempts to establish an American Bishopric.

In the election year of 1768 when George Clinton was elected to the Assembly, only one candidate of the Livingston faction who ran for office in the commercial counties secured a seat in the Assembly. The de Lancey-mercantile-church combination felt very strongly that lawyers could not properly represent a commercial city, while the Anglican Church establishment opposed the Livingston faction because of their identification with the dissenting congregations.

But in Ulster County, "where the Episcopalians were few and the lesser dissenting sects numerous, where there were few merchants or great land-holding aristocrats of the de Lancey faction and many independent farmers ... of Scotch-Irish and German descent," it should come as no surprise that George Clinton, a Presbyterian farmer and lawyer, was elected to the Assembly by the Ulsterites, and the reasons that Clinton was elected were varied.

In the years prior to Clinton's election to the General Assembly, the British imposed a new colonial policy, which threatened the economic welfare of the colonies, especially New York, and caused widespread protest and unrest. No doubt Clinton was familiar with the protests against the Stamp Act, and the results that the protests had had in the repeal of the act. He probably also understood that the general result of the Stamp Act episode, whereby mobs rioted in

New York City and proclaimed that "they disavowed every authority that is not derived from their representatives," was to create a broad, ill-defined distinction between the conservative and the radical elements in the population, giving the latter a taste for political agitation. As one observer said, "The late furious and audacious behavior of New Yorkers [was] exerted and supported by several Patriots of Consequence ... I am one ... acting on a principle of regard to the welfare of the Colonies, well knowing the Discords in which they would be speedily involved, if they were able to effect that Democratical system which is their sole aim, and which they may hereafter compass unless a timely check is given to that spirit of Libertinism and Independence, daily gaining ground through the ... conduct of a few pretended Patriots but in reality Enemies to the British Constitution."

Even though the Stamp Act was repealed, the following years saw the emergence of acute economic problems in the colony of New York, creating a renewed protest by the people against the British government and the royal governor. The inhabitants of Ulster County were similarly affected by the economic situation, and as we will see later, Clinton worked in the Assembly to relieve the financial stringency that confronted the poor in Ulster County.

In the winter of 1767, Parliament passed three acts that became very unpopular in the colonies. The first authorized the king to place commissioners in the colonies to collect duties. The second, the Townshend Act, laid certain duties on the importation of glass, lead, painter's colors, tea, and paper, the proceeds of which would go to the administration of justice in the colonies. The third, the regulatory act, suspended the legislative privileges of the New York Assembly until provision was made that the king's troops would be furnished with all the necessities required by law. As the delegate from Ulster County, Clinton echoed the anger of his constituents toward these unpopular acts.

In addition to these acts, the economic need for a new issue of legal paper money was prominent in 1768. However, in an act passed by Parliament in 1764, Parliament declared that "paper bills of credit, hereafter to be issued in any of His Majesty's colonies," will be prevented from being legal tender in payment of debts. By November of 1768, nearly all the paper money was sunk, and this action, coupled with the Townshend duties, caused a money stringency throughout the colony of New York, especially among the poorer classes. It was during this period of distress that property value declined, merchants had difficulty in finding means to pay the duties or meet their obligations in England, non-importation of British goods began in August of 1768, and the governor pressed for the granting of funds for the support of His Majesty's troops in the colony of New York.

Only by understanding the previously mentioned political, social and economic conditions that prevailed in New York during the 1760s can we more fully comprehend the reasons for Clinton's election to the General Assembly and his attachment to the Livingston faction. Due to the fact that the majority of Ulsterites in 1768 were Dissenters

(Presbyterians, Dutch Reformed, Methodists) rather than Anglicans, independent farmers rather than great landowning aristocrats or merchants, and less dependent on the favors of the royal governor than the de Lancey-mercantile-Anglican faction of the southern New York counties, the inhabitants of Ulster County selected George Clinton as their delegate to the General Assembly rather than the lieutenant governor's son, Cadwallader Colden, Jr.

The election of George Clinton to the Assembly culminated primarily as a rebuff to Lieutenant Governor Colden's insistence that Clinton should not be elected. Colden asked Charles Clinton to tell his son not to run, hoping that "George Clinton would leave those Northern radicals." However, the people of Ulster County, effected as they were by the political, social, and economic environment in which they lived, chose rather to repudiate the governor's and the de Lanceyite's candidate and select a "fiery young radical" from Kingston named Charles DeWitt, and a twenty-eight, year-old lawyer, George Clinton, in a contest that was "exceedingly bitter and exciting, so much so that fights were frequent over it, while social relations of strong standing were broken off."

For a lawyer and surveyor, prominently established and prospering, the idea of spending several months away from his livelihood could be disastrous. Clinton, however, traveled to New York City to be present when the new Assembly met in the city hall on October 27, 1768. Yet, in the Assembly, Clinton did not distinguish himself as a radical, urging the severance of ties to England by force, or as an advocate of the philosophical ideas of "democracy." For all intents and purposes, Clinton acted the role of the practical politician, advocating bills for the benefit of his constituents, compromising where necessary, and adhering to the Livingston resistance toward the whims of the dominant de Lanceyite faction.

Clinton played no great part in his first Assembly. He joined the Assembly in New York City in October 1768, in time to register a protest against the Townshend duties on November eighth. To pay his debt of gratitude to his constituents, he introduced a bill that became law on December 31, 1768, for the relief of the poor in Ulster County, providing for the election of overseers of the poor. As previously stated, the financial stringency that prevailed in 1768 as a result of the crown's suspension of legal paper money seriously affected the poorer classes. Clinton, opposed to the governor's suspension of bills of credit, strived therefore to aid his constituents by obtaining support for the relief of the poor.

On the last date of 1768, Clinton was present when the Assembly entered into its journal various resolves condemning the economic policy of Parliament, stating that it had become worse, and voiced a genuine concern over the security of the colony's political privileges. Governor Moore, dissolving the Assembly on January 2, 1769, wrote to the Earl of Hillsborough "that the present misconduct of the Assembly is entirely attributed to their violent measures," and did not meet the expectations of the royal governor.

In the January elections of 1769, the voters of the colony returned an Assembly that was predominently de Lanceyite. Both Schuyler and Clinton were returned to their seats in the Assembly and continued to occupy prominent positions among their Livingston friends. Clinton was often a resounding voice in this session of the Assembly, advocating, suggesting or introducing measures for the benefit of Ulsterites. He introduced bills to prevent damage by swine in Orange County and parts of Ulster, for better roads for Ulster, and for the regulation of the use of spiritous liquors at Ulster vendues.

In accordance with supporting bills for the benefit of his constituents, Clinton voted for bills that would relieve the lesser Protestant sects from discrimination of various kinds. Being from rural New York, where dissenters were numerous, Clinton believed that these groups, although differing in beliefs, should be permitted to practice their religion free from undue restraint.

From 1770 to 1773, Clinton continued to advocate bills for the benefit of the people of Ulster County. He secured such acts as those to regulate and keep in repair the public highways, to regulate the inns and taverns, to appoint inspectors of flour and beef packers, to prevent use of spiritous liquors at vendues, and to prevent the destruction of deer by bloodhounds or beagles in Ulster County.

Throughout his early career as a member of the New York Assembly, Clinton displayed his strong ties and allegiance to the minority Livingston faction. Although Clinton was not related to the Livingstons by his marriage, he nevertheless did attach himself by marriage to the socially and politically prominent Dutch families of Tappan and Wynkoop of Ulster County, who were ardent opponents of the crown and Parliament and future patriots in the Revolution. Clinton's most intimate associates in the Assembly were essentially those men related to the Livingstons by marriage; men such as Van Dam, Schuyler, Van Rensselaer, Beekman, Smith, and Ten Broeck.

Clinton became more closely attached to the Livingston faction as a result of the de Lanceyite-Anglican victory in January elections of 1769. "Our election is ended," wrote Peter Van Schaack, a prominent de Lanceyite and future loyalist in the Revolution, "and the Church triumphant. Messrs. Cruger, de Lancey, Walton and Jauncey were the members [for New York County], in spite of all the efforts of the Presbyterian interest combined with some other dissenting sects. This is what the Churchmen call a complete victory; 'tis a lasting monument to the power of the mercantile interest." After the election, Clinton joined forces with the Livingstons in the Assembly to defend Lewis Morris, the newly-elected Livingston delegate from Westchester County, and Morris's right to his seat in the Assembly.

With the de Lanceyites opposed to the selection of Lewis Morris, George Clinton and Philip Schuyler organized and led the Livingstons in an ill-fated attempt to prevent Morris's being unseated as the duly-elected representative from Westchester. During the proceedings, Clinton declared, "Is it not true that Colonel Morris is a resident of the Borough?" But the speaker, John Cruger, retorted that "such a question should not be put." Even though Morris lost his seat in the Assembly, being replaced by John de Lancey, "Clinton and Schuyler nevertheless distinguished themselves" as leaders of the Livingston opposition, especially "upon the question urging the absurdity of a different interpretation of the same words in the law relating to the elector and elected."

Not only did the de Lanceyites remove Lewis Morris from the Assembly, but they also effectively dismissed Philip Livingston, claiming that both Livingston and Morris were not bona fide residents of their constituencies. By the Livingstons, led by Clinton and Schuyler, failing in their attempt to maintain Morris's or Livingston's seat in the Assembly, their effective strength dwindled to eight, compared to their opponents' eighteen. This small group of Livingstons, which included DeWitt of Ulster, Ten Broeck of the Manor of Rensselaerwyck, Ten Eyck of Albany, Woodhull of Suffolk, Minderse of Schenectady Township, Pierre Van Cortlandt of the Cortlandt Manor, and Clinton and Schuyler, continued to remain intact and opposed to the de Lanceyites until the final session of the Assembly in the spring of 1775.

As an individual member of the Assembly, Clinton earnestly opposed the granting of funds for the support of British troops in the colony of New York, but when the situation demanded a change in philosophy, Clinton readily compromised where necessary. It must be remembered that Clinton was a practical man, and throughout his tenure as a member of the New York Assembly, he would alter his views for a greater end.

An outstanding case in point was the willingness of Clinton to vote for bills to financially support British troops in New York until 1773 in order to secure the issuing of legal bills of credit.

As previously mentioned, a severe financial stringency occurred in the colony of New York in 1769 and the winter of 1770 as a result of the non-importation agreement of 1768 and the suspension of nearly all legal bills of credit. Although smugglers violated the non-importation agreement during the period from 1768 to 1770, the imports of New York declined from L 428,000 in 1768 to L 74,000 in 1769, causing a great loss of money among the honest traders that signed the agreement. The need for currency prevailed throughout the colony as can be noted in the letters from Governor Moore and Lieutenant Governor Colden to the Earl of Hillsborough in July of 1769. "A paper currency would be of infinite advantage to the province by enabling it to grant the proper supplies [for the troops]; all our funds are exhausted, and the scarcity of money so great that a farm of 60 acres of land with a dwelling house and ... improvements ... shall be sold ... for ten pounds."

Amid the financial crisis that confronted the colony, Clinton and Schuyler in April of 1769 declared that they opposed the granting of funds for the support of the British troops. But when a bill, strongly urged by the governor, was proposed to secure relief from the currency stringency, providing for the emittance of L 120,000 in bills of credit, Clinton and Schuyler altered their statement and revealed that funds for the support of the troops would be given "our most serious consideration." Even though Clinton voted on December 15, 1769, not to grant L 2,000 for the support of the British troops, he oddly enough voted on the same day for a bill to grant L 2,000 for the support of the troops when the bill for emission of bills of credit, then pending, became law.

The passage of this L 2,000 grant revived the enthusiasm and the hostility of the Sons of Liberty, provoking a member of the organization to write and distribute a handbill entitled *To The Betrayed Inhabitants of the City and Colony of New York.* The inflammatory handbill charged the Assembly with having betrayed the liberties of the country by their disgraceful concession to the crown to keep themselves in power and prevent dissolution; de Lancey in particular was denounced for having formed a coalition with Governor Colden for the purpose of maintaining his influence in the Assembly.

The Assembly ordered Alexander MacDougall, the author of the handbill, to be brought before them under an indictment for libel, for which he was being tried in the courts. Having no counsel, Clinton intervened to ensure that MacDougall's remarks might be heard. The Assembly, seemingly becoming the judge in MacDougall's case while civil courts were trying him, attempted to pass judgment. Clinton rose and spoke fervently for the defendant. He admitted that the Assembly could deal with a prisoner as it chose, but that the public in the end would pass judgment and might well doubt the justice of any summary proceedings. He asked whether the Assembly was a party to the suit against MacDougall. Clinton urged, finally, that the true dignity of the Assembly might be "better supported by justice than by any overstrained authority." The de Lanceyites, however, showed no mercy, and committed MacDougall to jail.

Although Clinton voted against the decision to convict MacDougall, he nevertheless voted with the entire Assembly on the motion that charged that the handbill written by MacDougall was a "false, seditious, and infamous libel." Only Philip Schuyler voted no to the motion. Needless to say, Clinton compromised on this issue, and from July of 1770, when the act to emit L 120,000 in bills of credit was secured, until the spring of 1773, George Clinton supported not only every provisioning bill for the support of British troops, but also introduced a bill that continued the "granting to His Majesty the several duties and Impositions on Goods, Wares, and Merchandizes imported into this colony".

During his first sessions in the New York Assembly, Clinton revealed his strong attachment to the Livingston faction, supporting their measures against the whims of the de Lanceyites. Though he did not favor the financing of British troops in the colony, he nonetheless compromised on his belief in order to provide his constituents and the inhabitants of New York with currency. The needs of his constituents seemed to occupy most of his attention, which, for a newly-elected representative, would appear to be necessary and proper. In the legislative sessions from 1770 to March of 1773, Clinton seems to have taken his duties seriously and urged others to do so. In March 1771, he wrote to DeWitt, four days after the Assembly had been called by the governor:

> Dear Charles: Don't you think it Lightly derogatory
> to the honor, power and dignity of the body of the
> representatives of the good people of this colony, that
> a majority of their members should not attend, and a

minority attend agreeable to adjournment, adjourn
over from day to day for a whole week without being
able to do any business, this is the case however and
while you think of it tremble, you know you are one
of the delinquents.

As we have seen, Clinton was by no means a radical in New
York politics, but rather a sober politician, cognizant of the wishes
of his constituents and, as in the future, firm in his support of the
Livingston faction.

CHAPTER THREE

The Minority Leader

George Clinton: Minority Leader in
the New York General Assembly

The New York Assembly convened in January of 1773, unhampered by any strained relations with Great Britain. In all cases, the atmosphere that prevailed in the colony in early 1773 resembled the atmosphere of self-government and indirect rule that existed between Great Britain and New York prior to 1763 with the exception that the colony continued to grant funds for the support of His Majesty's troops. The British demand to support the troops in the colony, however, seems to have bothered no one in the Assembly and, from 1770 until 1773, every provisioning bill passed without opposition.

As the Assembly transacted its business during this session, Clinton emerged as a prominent figure in the Livingston faction. Even though Clinton did not champion any widespread reform of local institutions or advocate the extension of individual rights and liberties, his status and respect as a leader of the Livingstonians increased. Clinton's rise to the position of an outspoken, but local, patriotic figure, opposed to the granting of funds to British troops, opposed to the financial and coercive politics of the British government, but likewise opposed to any idea of independence or separation from the mother country, demands a careful evaluation in order to understand George Clinton's actions and career that led him toward his decision for American independence.

Clinton had previously opposed the granting of funds to support His Majesty's troops, but he never voted against the appropriation until 1773. Clinton's reasons for voting against the appropriation for L 1,000 in February of 1773 and his disinterestedness in the need for troops seemingly stemmed from the fact that the lower classes were fairly prosperous and contented, the Sons of Liberty were no longer heard of, and as cordial relations as had ever existed between the colony of New York and the mother country prevailed throughout the colony. Whatever the reason, only three members of the Assembly -- Clinton, Woodhull of Suffolk County, and de Noyelles of Orange County -- saw fit to vote against the appropriation. Most of the members of the Assembly saw and had a genuine need for the troops either to secure their trade, to control riotous mobs, or to check the sporadic uprisings of renters and tenants, antagonistic toward the proprietor's rent and taxation.

On February 19, 1773, several members of the de Lancey camp joined Clinton in opposing the purchase of field pieces for the British troops. Several weeks later, more de Lanceyites surprisingly joined Clinton, Woodhull, and Seaman in nearly defeating a bill that called for an appropriation of an additional L 800 for the troops. Clinton's determination for the return to self-government and the indirect rule that prevailed in the colony prior to 1763 became more intense as news reached America that Parliament had passed a law demanding a tax on tea entering the American colonies.

Relative calm persisted throughout New York from 1770 until 1773 in regard to agitation against British policy. The Townshend duties -- except the duty on tea -- had been repealed, and the trade acts had been modified in a manner that was acceptable to the colonists. However, when the East India Company received permission in 1773 to export tea free of all duties, but bearing a tax in America, the colonists objected, denouncing the law as a political trick designed to have the colonists pay a tax they advocated as unconstitutional. From this point until the fall of 1775, George Clinton became a forceful and outspoken leader in the Livingston faction, determined in his repudiation of the policies of the tyrannical British ministry, yet firm in his demand for reconciliation and harmony between Great Britain and the American colonies.

In the fall of 1773, the *New York Journal* spoke the mind of the inhabitants of the colony of New York, denouncing the tax on tea as an "obvious political trick, which would undermine the commerce of the colony by giving to the [East India] company a monopoly of trade, and threaten the liberty of the people by forcing them to pay an unconstitutional tax." William Smith wrote:

> A new flame is apparently kindling in America. We have intelligence that the E.I. Co. resolved to send tea to America to be sold, they paying the duty on importation ... Now the Sons of Liberty and the Dutch smugglers set up the cry of Liberty ... virtue and vice being thus united I suppose we shall repeat all the confusions of 1765 and 1766 ... Our domestic parties will probably die and be swallowed up in the general opposition to the Parliamentary project of raising the arm of government by revenue laws.

As Smith stated, the radical Sons of Liberty were joined by the conservative merchants and the New York Assembly in a rare, united front against the law permitting the importation of tea. The

Assembly's protest against the British measures culminated in the appointment of a standing committee of correspondence in January of 1774, composed of John Cruger, John de Lancey, Jauncey, Walton (delegates of the city and county of New York), Benjamin Seaman, Philipse, Kissam, Rapalje, Boerum, de Noyelles, Wilkins, Zebolun Seaman, and George Clinton. The upshot of the tea episode in the colonies brought about the direction of affairs in many of the colonies more and more under the control of extra-legal committees, causing the radicals and the unfranchised to play a much more prominent part in future contests.

There is no documentation to indicate that George Clinton favored any of the radical leaders' proposals to protest against the tea measures by using force or violence; nor is there an indication that Clinton espoused any new ideas to deal with the policies of the British government. Clinton remained steadfastly loyal to the Livingston faction in the General Assembly and continued his opposition toward any appropriation for His Majesty's troops.

In January of 1774, Clinton and a small minority supported the election of R. R. Livingston, a judge in the supreme court, as the duly-elected representative from the Manor of Livingston, even though Clinton believed and voted in 1775 for his view that judges should be independent of the people and not members of the Assembly. One month later, Clinton opposed the de Lanceyite accusation that Peter R. Livingston was not qualified to be a member of the General Assembly. During this same session of the Assembly, the de Lanceys attempted to gain further control in the colony by filling the positions of court justices with members of their family. Clinton, urged by his close friend, William Smith, to support the governor in these instances in opposition to the strong de Lancey control, succeeded in splitting the de Lanceyite supporters on this particular issue.

Although Clinton came forth as a leader of the Livingstonians, he nevertheless remained one of a minority of three delegates that continued in 1774 to oppose the L 2,000 appropriations for the support of the British troops in the colony. But, after shiploads of tea had been "quietly" dropped into the waters of New York harbor and the protests of the merchants had been made against the British measures, the Assembly adjourned on March 19, 1774, with Clinton returning to his home at New Windsor. Apparently, Clinton's actions as a leader of the Livingstons impressed many of the delegates, for in a letter to Philip Schuyler after adjournment, William Smith wrote:

> We have finished a long and disagreeable Session which I wish you had taken a Part not because I wish you Trouble but that you might have shared in the credit which Clinton has acquired in the Course of it.

By returning to New Windsor in March of 1774, George Clinton consequently played no direct part in the rise of the extra-legal committees in New York City or in the demand for a Continental Congress, which were to dominate politics in New York and in the colonies for the next two years.

While Clinton remained at home during the period from March 1774, until the opening session of the General Assembly on January 10, 1775, Parliament proceeded to put into effect the Coercive or "Intolerable" Acts against the inhabitants of Boston and Massachusetts. The thoughts of Peter Van Schaack clearly reveal the hostility of New Yorkers and the colonists toward these acts. "The measures of government, so strongly indicating a determination to establish the supremacy of Parliament over these colonies, are truly alarming. An appeal to the sword I am afraid is inevitable but palliating measures might have kept it off for a long time. The mutual interests of both should have restrained either from hastening the crisis, but I am afraid the die is cast. An absolute exemption from Parl. taxation in every case whatever, is what the colonies will never recede from. Indeed, if that is not their right, they do not enjoy the privileges of British subjects. That it is their right, is a concession we cannot expect from England, until necessity shall compel them to do it."

The news of these acts, which closed the port of Boston, reduced the local and provincial powers of self-government in Massachusetts, permitted royal officers to be tried in other colonies or in England when accused of crimes, and demanded the quartering of troops in the colonists' barns and empty houses, aroused widespread indignation in New York, immediately causing a number of merchants and the Body of Mechanics of New York City to form a committee of twenty-five and demand a return to the radical policy of non-importation.

Even though the radical and conservative elements in New York City opposed the Boston Port Act, the conservative merchants emphatically denounced the radical proposals of complete non-intercourse and non-importation as means of protesting against the "intolerable" acts. The conservatives, remembering the adverse financial effects of the non-importation act of 1768, chose rather to form a larger extra-legal committee composed of fifty-one members instead of twenty-five to represent the wishes of the people of New York. Inasmuch as the formation of the committee of fifty-one on May 23, 1774, clearly represented a victory for the conservative ideas of reconciliation, exclusion of the unfranchised and their leaders from political supremacy, and modified non-intercourse (the non-importation of such commodities only as were or might in the future be taxed by the British government), the committee ultimately agreed to the necessity of an immediate election and assembling of a general Continental Congress to represent a united voice of the colonies against the policies of the British government.

In the election of delegates to the First Continental Congress from New York, several counties authorized the New York delegates to act for them. In Ulster County, meetings were held at Kingston and New Windsor, which approved of the delegates for the city and county of New York. "Wednesday last, August 31, 1774, a great number of inhabitants of Ulster County had a meeting and agreed in sentiment with their brethren in New York and did not intend sending delegates to Philadelphia."

Apparently, George Clinton and his constituents favored the conservative view for a faithfully observed non-importation agreement and a reconciliation between Great Britain and the colonies that the delegates from the city and county of New York -- Philip Livingston, Isaac Low, John Jay, John Alsop, and James Duane -- were instructed to advocate at the Congress. Although Colden wrote to Dartmouth that "the present Political zeal and frenzy is almost entirely confined to the City of New York [and] the people in the Counties are in no ways disposed to become active, or to bear any Part in what is proposed by the Citizens [of New York City]," the farmers of Ulster and the other river counties were nevertheless quietly sympathetic toward the forces at work in the Continental Congress.

The First Continental Congress convened at Carpenter's Hall in Philadelphia on September 5, 1774, and proceeded to endorse the Suffolk (Massachusetts) Resolutions, to adopt an Association to enforce the non-intercourse policy, and to provide that those who refused to follow the resolves of the Congress should be punished by social ostracism, commercial boycott, and confiscation of property. As a result of the enactment of the Association, the political scene in New York underwent a significant change; the inhabitants began to realign themselves into loyalist and patriot parties. "The term loyalist ... must be confined to those who were prepared to side with England when for them it became a choice between submitting to Parliament or to Congress, just as the term [patriots] must be confined to those who were prepared to side with Congress under the same conditions."

The loyalists of the colony of New York, led mainly by Episcopalian clergymen and the de Lanceyite faction, denied the authority of Congress, denied the expediency of non-intercourse, declared that their organization was the English government itself, and labeled the powers of Congress as a tyranny far more oppressive than the alleged tyranny of Parliament. By withdrawing from the extra-legal movement, the loyalists were forced to rely on the Assembly in order to obtain a redress of grievances and a suppression of the extra-legal movement.

While the Congress petitioned the crown and threatened peaceful coercion, many New Yorkers prepared for war. In several counties, the patriots formed committees to enforce the Association. In Ulster County, where the people had previously sympathized with the Bostonians by sending to them four or five hundred barrels of flour (some of which was ground and packed by George Clinton) in the fall of 1774, freeholders met from five towns at Hurley on January 6, 1775, to approve the Association and recommend that the towns appoint committees to enforce it. Such committees were appointed in Kingston, New Windsor, Hanover, Showangnuk, and Wallkill, and the loyalists of Ulster County, the most radical county in New York next to Suffolk, were threatened with tar and feathers.

Amid hostility that arose between the factions in the colony of New York, the General Assembly convened on January 10, 1775, and became the center of interest as it debated on confirming or refusing to confirm the actions of the First Continental Congress.

Prior to the opening of the New York Assembly in January of 1775, Clinton's status was not that of a prominent figure in the American colonies or in New York in the American cause for a redress of grievances and reconciliation with Great Britain. He was by no means a radical leader as were Isaac Sears and Alexander MacDougall, but rather a local figure, sympathetic toward the actions of the First Continental Congress. Not until the New York Assembly opened to transact its business did Clinton emerge as a leader in the Livingston or patriot party by urging and demanding that the Assembly approve the proceedings of the Continental Congress and its non-importation proposal, elect delegates to a Second Congress, and adopt a clear statement of grievances.

On January 26, when the Assembly voted to consider the work of the First Continental Congress, George Clinton showed his patriot colors. The motion failed, eleven to ten, with Clinton and the patriot minority receiving their first of many defeats at the hands of the dominant de Lanceyite-loyalist faction. The majority of this small minority of patriots were traditionally aligned with the Livingstonians and continued to remain intact throughout this session of the Assembly.

The resolutions to thank the delegates to the First Continental Congress, to thank the merchants for maintaining the non-intercourse agreement, and to appoint delegates to the Second Continental Congress, were similarly defeated by increasing majorities -- the last by a vote of seventeen to nine. Upon the defeat of these resolutions,

Clinton, according to a loyalist contemporary, gave his first hint of taking up arms. "He declared he would not draw his sword against his sovereign but upon the most cogent reasons, but insinuated that time was nearly come that the Colonies must have recourse to arms and the sooner the better." The Assembly had ignored the extra-legal movement altogether, believing that it was better to abandon the neighboring colonies than to desert Great Britain.

Obviously, Clinton maintained a different view concerning the means by which to obtain a redress of the grievances of the colonies.

To the de Lanceyite-loyalist faction, the extra-legal movement had become illegal and revolutionary, asserting claims to power and authority that the Assembly did not dare recognize. Loyalists throughout the colonies and in England hailed the resistance of the Assembly to the extra-legal movement. On the other hand, patriots angrily protested that the Assembly by no means represented the sentiments of the people of the province. Even Clinton's hostility toward the loyalist de Lanceyites erupted in March of 1775. According to William Smith, Clinton "stormed" at the loss of a bill and "disrupted the Whole House," claiming "that the city members and some others always got their bills past, and his were often refused." Although the loyalists and patriots in the New York Assembly disagreed on the authority and on the proposals of the First Continental Congress, they were essentially at one on the matter of grievances.

George Clinton, sympathetic to the colonial cause for a reconciliation between Great Britain and the colonies, and a redress of grievances, embarked on a struggle in the New York Committee on Grievances and in the New York Assembly to secure the adoption of the resolves and grievances of the First Continental Congress. Appointed to the committee on January 31, along with Schuyler, de Lancey, Brinkerhoff, Gale, Wilkins, Brush, Billop, Rapalje, Kissam, and Nicoll, Clinton simply echoed the proposals of the Congress and did not espouse any new ideas. He opposed "every idea of taxation, internal and external, for the purpose of raising a revenue on the subjects in America without their consent." Only Clinton and Schuyler voted against de Lanceyite resolution in the committee on grievances that stated that "His Majesty and the Parliament of Great Britain have a right to regulate the trade of the colonies, and to lay duties on articles that are imported directly into this colony from any foreign country or plantation, which may interfere with the products or manufactures of Great Britain or any other parts of His Majesty's dominions."

Clinton made his most resounding condemnation of ministerial policy during the debate on the Petition to the King, the Memorial to the Lords, and the Remonstrance to the Commons. "The ill-policied scheme of colony adm. pursued by your Majesty's ministers since the close of the last war, has been productive of great warmth in every part of your empire; nor can we avoid declaring that we view those acts with that jealousy which is the necessary result of a just sense of the blessings of freedom, and abhor the principles they contain, as establishing precedents subversive of the rights, privileges and property, and dangerous to the lives of your Majesty's American subjects."

By regulating the government of the province of Massachusetts and by discontinuing shipping within the harbor of Boston, the British government, Clinton argued, likewise had committed an act that affected the colony of New York. However, Clinton did not wish to apologize for any of the measures that Bostonians or other colonists enacted in order to obtain redress, and therefore demanded that such statements as the following be struck out of the statement of grievances.

> "At the same time we also must express our disappropriation of the violent measures that have been pursued in some of the colonies, which can only tend to increase our misfortunes, and to prevent our obtaining redress."

Rather, Clinton believed that, "although your Majesty's American subjects have, in some instances, submitted to the power exercised by the parent state, they nevertheless conceive themselves entitled to an equal participation of freedom with their fellow subjects in Britain." He would have proceeded to aid and support the patriot resistance movement in Boston in March of 1775, but said, "he will never put Arms at this Juncture into such Hands since he believes the Force would be under a Tory Influence and employed against the Liberty Boys in N. England."

The Assembly, with George Clinton concurring, agreed that the extension of the admiralty courts beyond their traditional limits to deny American subjects trial by jury, the prohibition of the emission of paper money, and the encouragement of Roman Catholicism in Quebec, were also grievances. The Assembly passed Clinton's proposal that judges in the colony "should hold their commissions during good behavior," and that the Assembly "would stand ready to give them such adequate and permanent salaries as will render them independent of the people." Clinton's opposition to the Quebec Act, however, failed to receive the support of the Anglicans in the Assembly. Believing that the "Roman Catholic Religion ... [was] A sanguinary religion, equally repugnant to the genuine simplicity of Christianity, and the maxims of sound philosophy," Clinton echoed the fear of the Protestants in the colonies that Catholicism and Anglicanism were about to merge, thereby subjecting Americans to the tyranny of the Pope and an American bishop who would presumably enforce Anglican authority upon all the various sects.

Although Clinton abhorred the policies of the British government, he nevertheless opposed disunion or separation from the British Empire. He consistently voted for resolutions that declared "Our commotions are honest struggles for maintaining our constitutional liberty, and not dictated by a desire for independence," or "Considering ourselves as an inseparable part of the British Empire ... we readily assent that public Expediency must, in some cases, induce a submission to the exercise of a supreme leg. Power, in the British Parliament."

However, he believed that the exercise of supreme legislative power "must never take place but in cases of absolute necessity, and where our own leg. is incompetent, and with a view to the general weal of the Empire in the Regulation of Commerce."

In other words, Clinton demanded a return to self-government and the policy of indirect rule that existed in the colonies prior to 1763. Self-government in New York and home rule in all the colonies occupied a place of utmost importance in Clinton's political thought, for the simple reason that indirect rule had become an accepted way of life in the British Empire. Supremacy of Parliament in all cases whatsoever pertaining to the affairs of the American colonies constituted a radical change in the social and political order, and to Clinton, a change that infringed on the rights, privileges, property, and lives of His Majesty's subjects in America.

Having formulated a Petition to the King, a Memorial to the Lords, and a Remonstrance to the Commons, the Assembly adjourned on April 3, 1775. Prior to adjournment, the Assembly appointed a standing committee of correspondence composed of both factions. As a leader of the minority Livingston or patriot party, Clinton obtained a place on the committee, and while he served on the committee, the people of Ulster County, as in other counties in New York, began to ignore the Assembly and turn to the Committee of Sixty as the real government of the province. Their first act of loyalty to the patriot movement commenced with the selection of delegates to represent Ulster County in the proposed New York Provincial Convention.

CHAPTER FOUR

The Drift Toward Independence

Second Continental Congress

With the refusal of the New York Assembly to appoint delegates to the Second Continental Congress, the Committee of Sixty moved to consider "the ways and means of causing delegates to be elected to meet the delegates of the other colonies ... in general Congress." In

March of 1775, the Committee issued a circular letter to all counties, asking them to consider the advisability of a Provincial Convention and to send delegates to such a convention that was to meet in New York City on April 20, 1775. Contrary to their position prior to the First Continental Congress, the freeholders and freemen of Ulster County decided that in 1775 they would select delegates and have a voice in the Second Continental Congress.

The struggle, where there was a struggle in the counties of New York for the election of delegates to the Provincial Convention, was mainly between those who favored a Second Congress and those who did not; between those who favored the patriot cause and those who traveled the path of loyalism. In Ulster County, thirty-nine deputies from ten towns, seemingly loyal to the patriot movement, assembled at New Paltz on April 7. They proceeded to name three delegates -- George DeWitt, Levi Pawling, and George Clinton.

The only opposition to the patriot, extra-legal committee movement in Ulster County seems to have stemmed from Cadwallader Colden, Jr., and Peter and Walter DeBois, protesting that the election was unlawful, and that Provincial Conventions, Continental Congresses, and local committees had "a direct tendency to Sap, undermine, and destroy our most excellent Constitution, and introduce a Republican Government with its Horrid concomitants, faction, Anarchy, and finally Tyranny." Colden became a victim of social ostracism, but his fear of the extra-legal movement in Ulster County did not produce any radical instructions for the delegates to follow at the Provincial Convention.

There had been no movement for independence in Ulster County when the delegates were selected to attend the Provincial Convention in April of 1775. The fact of the matter was that Clinton and the other delegates were instructed to follow and adhere to somewhat conservative instructions, calling for the "preserving of our Constitution and opposing the execution of ... oppressive acts of the Brit. Parl. until a reconciliation between G. B. and America on cons't principles can be obtained ... and to concert such measures as may tend to the preservation of the rights and Liberties of America." The delegates were also urged by the inhabitants to ask for a day of fasting so that the people could "implore Divine aid in restoring a happy reconciliation between the mother country and her Amer. colonies." Such instructions were by no means radical in nature, for as the Provincial Convention convened in New York City on April 20, 1775, radical leaders, men like Alexander MacDougall and John Lamb, demanded that the delegates to the Second Continental Congress should make an "unqualified, defiant assertion of American rights, ... whereas the conservative faction of the patriot party emphasized [as did the delegates from Ulster County] the hope for reconciliation with Great Britain."

The Provincial Convention met for only two days, but during that period, the delegates elected the old delegates of the First Continental Congress, with the exception of Isaac Low and John Haring, namely Philip Schuyler, Lewis Morris, R. R. Livingston, Francis Lewis and George Clinton, to represent the province of New York in the Second Continental Congress. For all intents and purposes, the five newly-elected delegates were traditionally aligned to the Livingston faction in New York politics. And William Smith recorded that, when the guns began to be fired and the news of the battle of Lexington reached New York on April 23, the parties had made their "fatal decisions;" the de Lanceyites had "irrevocably thrown their lot with the crown, while the Livingstons were completely committed to the cause of the Congress."

When the Provincial Convention adjourned on April 22, 1775, the delegates to the Second Continental Congress had been instructed to follow similar instructions that were favored by George Clinton and the other Ulster delegates -- to work for "the preservation and reestablishment of American Rights and Privileges, and for the Restoration of Harmony between Great Britain and the Colonies." But, even before the delegates packed their bags for the trip to Philadelphia, the news of Lexington and Concord traveled throughout the colonies. New York City was in the hands of the mob, business was at a standstill, and armed citizens paraded in the streets. Lord North's conciliatory resolution, that had unfortunately arrived in New York one day after the report from Lexington, aroused little enthusiasm, for by that time, the angered inhabitants had prepared for armed conflict, called for a Committee of One Hundred to enforce the Association and prorogue a Provincial Congress, and looked with interest toward the opening of the Second Continental Congress.

The delegates from New York arrived in Philadelphia on May 10, 1775, and proceeded to engage themselves in the business of conducting a war. Continental troops were raised, the militia organized, fortifications planned and erected, and ammunition and supplies secured. While accepting the battle of Lexington as a declaration of war, Congress appointed George Washington on June 17, "General and commander-in-chief of the army of the United Colonies." On July 6, Congress issued its declaration for the use of arms to oppose any attempt by Britain to "effect by force of arms what by law or right they could never effect." Even though the Congress detested the policies of the tyrannical British ministry and prepared to fight rather than submit to Parliament's laws, the hope for reconciliation still prevailed as the members moved to address a last petition to George III -- The Olive Branch Petition -- "intreating him to find means to promote a Negotiation for the Establishment of ... tranquility."

George Washington

George Clinton: Brigadier General

George Clinton had previously shown his hostility toward the British ministry and had urged the use of arms to obtain a redress of grievances in March of 1775. At Philadelphia during the summer of 1775, Clinton continued to speak "for the Cause of Liberty" rather than independence. There is no indication that Clinton favored or advocated independence at this time, for the simple reason that he was not recorded as speaking at all in the journal of the Second Continental Congress. The only thing that is certain at this time is that Clinton was primarily concerned with the preparations for the war effort in the colony of New York.

When the First Provincial Congress of New York adjourned on July 8, 1775, a Council of Safety was appointed and entrusted with the power to open letters to the Congress, examine suspected persons

(Loyalists), take measures to implement orders from the Continental Congress, appropriate money, and superintend military affairs. It was with this council that Clinton maintained close contact in the summer of 1775, primarily directing his correspondence to John McKesson, secretary to the Council of Safety and one of the most active Americans in New York during the Revolution.

Clinton seems to have been most concerned with the problems of raising money and supplying the New York troops with clothes and ammunition. McKesson reported to Clinton in June of 1775 that "the Colony has NO MONEY," and urged Clinton to "let your Omnipotent House give positive Directions ... if New York is to raise an army and supply everything for them." McKesson also proposed to Clinton that "I wish in your great Wisdom you could allow N. York Troops to be clothed ... as clothing and a little Bounty would induce better men to enlist."

Added to his task of aiding the war effort in New York, Clinton introduced several men to George Washington to serve in the continental army. In introducing men, such as "Mr. White of New Jersey," Clinton used various phrases that indicated his patriotic leanings; phrases like "inspired with Love for our much-injured Country," and "induced with a warm Friendship for the Cause of Liberty."

As a result of being stricken with a "severe sickness," apparently in late August of 1775, Clinton's work at the Second Continental Congress came to a halt. His illness seems to have incapacitated him until December of 1775. From all indications, Clinton must have been critically ill, for William Smith, writing in October of 1775, exclaimed: "I bless God, my dear Friend, for the Prospect of your Recovery, ... I shall receive you as risen from the grave." And later in 1775, Smith wrote in a letter to Clinton, "I am sure it afforded me the most singular Pleasure to discover the Interest you have in the Esteem of the Public by the manner in which People allow themselves when most men imagined from our accounts that you had taken Farewell of this vain and anxious Life." It was during this period of Clinton's illness that the prospect for reconciliation with Great Britain dimmed, and men began to speak of independence.

In October of 1775, news arrived in the colonies that the King had repudiated the Olive Branch Petition and had issued a proclamation declaring that the colonies were in a state of rebellion. The Continental Congress and the Provincial Congress of New York still followed a course of moderation, hoping that the British government would propose some scheme of reconciliation. But in the colony of New York, the economic situation in the fall of 1775 and the winter of 1776 forced many inhabitants either into the loyalist camp, that proposed to submit and open the ports to England, or into the radical camp, that advocated to open the ports of America to the world and declare independence.

The most significant factor that led toward independence in New York was the failure of the non-intercourse policy. During the year 1775, imports from England into the colonies fell from L 2,687,000 to L 213,000, and this action, coupled with non-exportation which became effective in September of 1775, drastically hindered commerce and prosperity in the colony of New York. "The economic distress in New York was such as to lead people to lend a ready ear to any proposal which looked towards a revival of prosperity." This coercive policy of non-intercourse, advanced by the Continental Congress, not only became self-defeating, but was also met by Parliament in December of 1775 with the Prohibitory Act, which closed the ports of the colonies to overseas trade and made no concessions except an offer to pardon repentant rebels. In essence, the Prohibitory Act rejected the last petition to the King -- the Olive Branch Petition -- and caused the colonists to choose between their rights as Americans or their King; a choice for most Americans that was not easy to make.

Clinton claimed, in a discussion with William Smith in July of 1778, that "he took his Resolution [favoring independence] upon the Rejection of the last petition [Olive Branch] offering to be at Peace upon being reduced to the State of 1763." Many other patriots, years after the Declaration of Independence, similarly stated that they, too, had taken their stand for independence upon learning that Parliament had enacted the Prohibitory Act.

In George Clinton's case, the facts will show that he did not publicly advocate independence at this or at any time prior to the Declaration of Independence, but rather vacillated in his views and drifted into independence.

In December of 1775, the Second New York Provincial Congress appointed George Clinton a brigadier general in the militia. Having recovered from his illness, Clinton proceeded to help organize and direct the war effort in New York. His thoughts concerning the relationship between Great Britain and the American colonies in January of 1776 seem to reflect the view that the war was being fought primarily to secure the rights and liberties denied to His Majesty's American subjects by the British ministry, rather than to advance the cause of independence. In writing to Colonel DeWitt, Clinton declared that "The season is approaching when in all probability you may be called upon to defend your County ag't the Attacks of a Tyrannical ministry and it will reflect great Dishonor on a County so forward in every Respect in the Cause of Liberty to be found so extremely negligent in so important a Matter ... as forming a Regim't in the Northern End of Ulster County." As Thomas Paine's pamphlet, *Common Sense*, circulated throughout the colonies, Clinton was actively engaged in organizing the defense of the Hudson River Highlands, and by March of 1776, the Second Continental Congress appointed him a brigadier general in the continental service, giving him command of the New York Highlands.

By the spring of 1776, the political factions, actually the division of ideas in New York, centered primarily in the ranks of the revolutionists themselves. The loyalists, though not suppressed, were driven "from the arena of politics into the arena of war." In the election for delegates to the Third Provincial Congress in April of 1775, the conservative patriots, led by the continental delegates, and the radicals, attached to the Mechanics' Committee of New

York City, fought over the issues of whether independence should be delayed or hastened, and whether the new state government should be reasonably "oligarchic" or broadly democratic.

The delegates from Ulster County to the Third Provincial Congress were instructed on May 16 to vote for George Clinton as a delegate to the Continental Congress. Sometime during this period before Clinton departed for Philadelphia, Clinton made a speech that indirectly favored independence. Discussing this period of time with George Clinton in 1778, William Smith commented, "I blamed him for his Heat -- reminded him of a Speech before the Decla. of Ind: that he would consent to go to Hell if he could drag Great Britain after him." But Smith also relates that "he [Clinton] had informed [us] of his Disinclination to the Disunion shortly before it [the speech] & when he was going to Philad." Clinton was without doubt firmly attached to the American cause for independence in 1778. But as Smith related, Clinton did have some misgivings about independence prior to the Declaration of Independence. Smith said, "[I] told him of Jay's Decla, that Ind. [independence] was the first and ought to be the last Object -- Showed him the Purport of the Decla. of Rights agt. the Powers of Parlt. & how the Delegates had explained disavowing Independency -- He [Clinton] said Jay was right."

On June 7, 1776, at the Continental Congress, Richard H. Lee of Virginia introduced his resolutions, proposing that the Continental Congress "declare the United Colonies free and independent states." Clinton's actions and thoughts during the debate on Lee's resolutions seem to have been directed toward the proceedings of the Third New York Provincial Congress. In the debate, Clinton and the other New York delegates took little part. Edward Rutledge, a delegate from South Carolina, reported that "Clinton has Abilities but is silent in general and wants [when he does speak] that Influence to which he is entitled. Floyd, Wisner, Lewis, and Alsop, though good men, never leave their chairs." The delegates were informed by the New York Provincial Congress that they had no authority to vote on the question of independence or on the question of a new government, for measures were under way to determine the sentiments of the people of New York in regard to a new government and to independence.

Clinton and the New York delegates did not vote for independence on July 2, for want of instructions from the Provincial Congress. In New York, elections were held in June for a Fourth Provincial Congress, but not until July 9, 1776, did this Congress vote for a declaration of independence.

By his actions in the Second Continental Congress prior to the vote for independence and his statements in the year 1776, George Clinton seems to have weighed his political actions very carefully. Portraying a vacillating politician, Clinton apparently wished to echo the demands of the majority of the inhabitants of the colony of New York. Though Clinton repudiated the policies of the British ministry and fought with determination to secure the rights of His Majesty's American subjects, he seems to have believed, as his actions indicate, that the decision for independence rested with the people and, if independence became inevitable as it did, he would go along with the decision. Throughout his career as an assemblyman in the colony of New York and as a delegate at the Continental Congress, George Clinton did not come to power as a leader for independence, but rather as a strong, military leader in New York.

CHAPTER FIVE

Election to the Governorship

The final decision for American independence touched every individual in New York. Independence had brought about the question of allegiance –- allegiance to England or loyalty to the new-born state. The loyalists, of which there were many in New York, had always feared the danger of complete separation, for their livelihood depended on a close, working relationship with the mother country. Most members of the Anglican-commercial-de Lanceyite faction had remained loyal to Great Britain, mainly due to their family and religious ties, their need for trade with other British ports, and their desire to maintain their prominent political status in New York.

On the other hand, the revolutionists in New York formulated a plan -- after the Declaration of Independence -- for a new state government. As we have seen, the revolutionists themselves were divided in respect to the formation of the new government. The radicals, entrenched in the Mechanics' committee, feared that the proposed constitution of the new state would resemble as near as possible the old form of government; whereas the conservatives, led by men like John Jay, had a corresponding fear that the new government would be "too weak at the top and too broadly democratic at the bottom."

Most of Clinton's time was occupied with the war in New York and its administration, leaving him very little time to aid in forming the state constitution. By July 14, 1776, Clinton was at Fort Montgomery and Fort Constitution in the New York Highlands, and in August of 1776, his command was enlarged to include the counties of Dutchess, Ulster, Orange, and Westchester. In the following year prior to his election as governor of the state of New York, Clinton remained in the New York Highlands, directing the war and gaining the admiration of the soldiers and the inhabitants that served under his command. But, to show the reasons for Clinton's election to the governorship in June of 1777 will go a long way in explaining the attitude of the inhabitants of New York toward the type of leader they desired to conduct the affairs of the new-born state.

Clinton played only an insignificant role in the New York Convention of 1776-1777 that framed and adopted the state's first constitution. Even though the war occupied most of Clinton's time, he did manage to attend the Provincial Convention on April 11, 1777, to vote for Jay's proposal to the state constitution for a council of appointment, whereby the governor's power to appoint officials would be limited. The basic struggle in the New York Convention centered around the thoughts of the conservative and radical factions.

The conservatives advocated a balanced and a rather aristocratic form of government, whereas the radicals demanded a highly popular foundation; one in which the legislature, directly representing the people, would dominate the executive and judicial branches, while property qualifications for the ballot would be low or absent. The radicals opposed special social, economic, or religious privileges, and attacked the church establishment, primogeniture, entail, methods of taxation favoring the rich, and discrimination against new settlements in the apportionment of representatives.

It is perhaps essential to note at this time that the final constitution, framed in the midst of revolution, was one in which "the conservatives were successful ... securing a government measurably centralized and measurably aristocratic." However, "we know that there was considerable pressure for a more democratic form, and as John Jay mentioned, 'Another turn of the winch would have cracked the cord'." Jay's "turn of the winch" refers to the accepted possibility that, had a popular vote been taken, the constitution would have been "cracked" by the wave of democratic feeling that prevailed throughout the state. The new constitution, drawn and adopted by a group of provincial lawyers, farmers, and proprietors, was nevertheless proclaimed on April 22, 1777, from a platform mounted on a hogshead in front of the courthouse at Kingston, with state-wide elections for governor and other elected officials slated for June.

With the election for governor set for June of 1777, various candidates, endowed with prominent family connections, property, and political appeal, were recognized for the office. Of the candidates mentioned, John Jay, Philip Schuyler, John Morin Scott, and George Clinton, all were members of the New York aristocracy, with Clinton a man of modest wealth. Jay, a graduate of Kings College, a successful lawyer, and a conservative, was not doubted in his patriotism, but his feelings toward democracy were certainly questioned. Schuyler, a rich, wealthy patriot, who lent his services greatly in the colonial assembly, had little or no sympathy for the democratic urges of the times. On the other hand, John Morin Scott was a thorough-going democrat. He was a graduate of Yale College, a prominent Son of Liberty, and, like Clinton, a Presbyterian, but he was so radical that he held little appeal to the moderates.

Clinton did very little to advance his own cause for the governorship. Actually, it seems that Clinton's greatest asset was the fact that he continued to direct the war effort in New York, for by doing so, he became a popular, well-respected, military leader. Clinton was so well respected as a military figure that the militia at the forts in New York asked for and received leave to vote for him. "It was known that these officers and soldiers were opposed to the Livingstons and that they preferred Clinton their General to Philip Livingston who was then talked of for Govr. and they partitioned for Leave to vote at the Forts."

As the election for governor drew to a close in June and July of 1777, news circulated that George Clinton and Philip Schuyler, both of whom were generals in New York, led in the balloting. A Mrs. Montgomery wrote to William Smith that "her brother is uncertain whether Schuyler or Clinton is the elective Govr. -- Below in Dutchess, Ulster and Orange they have voted for the latter." She also reported that "above [the northern counties] but few people attended the Elections ... The Northern Inhabitants have been shy to the New Model [state government]."

Concerning the election itself, only the returns from six counties have been preserved. The ballots from Orange and the southern counties presumably were destroyed. Of the total vote in six counties, Schuyler received 1012 ballots to 865 for Clinton. Clinton must have received a large southern county vote, for the final returns showed Jay with 397 votes, Scott 368, Schuyler 1199, and Clinton 1828. It is interesting to note that Clinton may have received many more votes, but "in voting for governor, many threw in Votes for Genl. Clinton," which meant that "all these [votes] tho' probably intended for George are lost for James [Clinton] is the oldest General." Clinton also received 1647 votes for lieutenant governor, defeating his closest rival, Pierre Van Cortlandt, who amassed 1098 votes. Not until September 1, did the legislature elect a lieutenant governor, finally awarding the post to Pierre Van Cortlandt.

There is little doubt that the colonists who fought with Clinton supported or voted for any other candidate except Clinton. That the soldier-vote aided Clinton and that they respected him as a dedicated leader cannot be denied. One of Clinton's New England soldiers wrote,

"Never had a man more absolute Ascendancy over people, than he has over the Inhabitants of this part of the Country -- They are now gathered round their Chief ... in high spirits -- exulting in their behavior at Fort Montgomery and wishing for another opportunity ... Their Governor deservedly has their Esteem -- few men are his Superiors."

The election of George Clinton to the governorship caused some misgivings among the wealthy aristocrats. Schuyler, in learning that Clinton had been elected, wrote to Jay, "I hope General Clinton's having the chair of Government will not cause any divisions amongst the friends of America. Altho his family and connections do not entitle him to so distinguished a predominance; yet he is virtuous and loves his country, has abilities and is brave, and hope will experience from every patriot what I am resolved he shall have from me, support, countenance, and comfort." Although the wealthy families of the new state believed that they should control the state since British dominance had ceased to exist, the inhabitants apparently saw the need to have a strong, military man, devoted to his homeland, lead the new state during these years of war. Similarly, Washington seems to have been pleased by Clinton's election. "The appointment of General Clinton to the Government of your State is an event, that, in itself, gives me great pleasure, and very much abates the regret I should otherwise feel for the loss of his Services in the Military line. That Gentleman's Character is Such, as will make him peculiarly useful at the Lead of your State, in a situation so alarming and interesting, as it at present experiences."

George Clinton's ascent to power as governor did not result from the support of a strong, popular, political coalition. Likewise, his election cannot be attributed to the belief that the voters favored a devoted, thorough-going democrat and early advocate of independence, for as we have seen, Clinton did not display these characteristics. He did not champion widespread reform of local institutions or the extension of individual rights and liberties. George Clinton simply evolved and was elected as a military hero, as a defender of the land.

After taking the oath of office on July 30, 1777, Clinton did not call the legislature into session until September 1777, where on September 10, he delivered his first inaugural address. In this brief yet concise speech, Clinton outlined the problems that confronted his war-ridden state and also advocated several measures, primarily a revision of the state's military laws, and a demand for giving attention to the floundering state of finances. Even at this point in his career, Clinton was still entirely occupied with the military affairs relating to the defense of the Highlands, but as the war continued, "Mr. Clinton ... resolved to risk everything for Independency." Clinton became a product of the American movement for independence, professing to be a "Child of the People, and would [if necessary] die in the cause."

CHAPTER SIX

New York's First Governor

George Clinton: First Governor
of the State of New York

Indeed, it was the floundering state of the state's finances that concerned Clinton as he began his opening remarks during his first inaugural address as governor. Paper money was alarming to Clinton in 1777 due to the fact that New York had put so much paper into circulation in 1775-1776 but failed to provide a sinking fund.

Price regulation was attempted to control the debt but failed. Therefore, Clinton urged that a sinking fund be established to combat this debt, "which if neglected, will not only prove burdensome to the state, but strike at the credit of our currency, which it behooves us so much to support." Undoubtedly, merchants, manufacturers, and large landowners would have the most to lose, principally in the obtaining of credit if the value of the currency in the state diminished. Clinton, a political animal, realized the importance of aristocratic support as well as the necessity of obtaining their produce for the war effort. Thus, he espoused the need for a sound and stable currency; a need that occupied his political and economic thought throughout his reign as governor.

A distinct part of the governor's political philosophy was also revealed in his opening address to the legislature. He urged that the separation of the three branches of government should not be ignored, but that members of government should "remain within the several departments in which the constitution has placed us, and thereby preserve the same inviolate, and repay the trust reposed in us by our constituents when they made us the guardians of their rights." He emphasized that "it shall always be my strenuous endeavor on the one hand to retain and exercise for the advantage of the people the powers with which they have invested in me; on the other, carefully to avoid the invasion of those rights which the constitution has placed in their persons." In his opening address, then, Clinton's thoughts reveal his genuine concern for the people, especially the burden confronting all the people over the paper money problem; and secondly, his belief in the importance of the separation of powers in government.

It was one of Clinton's principal policies to stamp out disaffection and loyalism in the state, and in general, he was successful. The governor approved wholeheartedly of vigorous anti-Tory measures, primarily because New York had a larger proportion of Tories in its population than any other state. Under the governor's urging, the Committee for Detecting and Defeating Conspiracies engaged in a crusade against the Tories. Loyalist property was seized and sold for the benefit of the state treasury. The Confiscation Act of 1779, approved by Clinton, caused fifty-nine prominent Loyalists to lose their estates. In 1780, estates were sold, after being divided into small holdings, which began a revolution in land tenures in the state.

Finally, as a result of the Trespass Act of 1783, thirty to forty thousand Loyalists were driven out of the state to Canada, Nova Scotia, and England; and those Tories who remained were disenfranchised in 1784. For Clinton, he "had rather roast in Hell to all eternity, than consent to a dependence upon Great Britain or show mercy to a damned Tory." However, apparently the majority of New Yorkers approved of the governor's actions, and on the whole, the treatment of the Loyalists by the revolutionists, all things taken into consideration, was moderate and fair.

Throughout Clinton's career as governor of New York State, he was a firm believer in state's rights; that is, that the state, covering a small land mass, would be better able to deal with the problems of the people, and would have a genuine obligation to the demands of the people than any national authority far removed from the intimate, prevailing conditions confronting local governments. However, the governor was similarly conscious of the need for a unifying national effort to coordinate the forces to win the war and was indignant toward the congress for failing to provide the essential leadership and programs. He writes in March of 1778:

> I wish the defects of a certain great body (Congress) were less apparent. Even their Want of Wisdom but too evident in most of their measures would in that Case be less injurious. A New Mode of doing Business by proxy is very fashionable whenever any alarming Difficulties arise. They are referred to the New B of W and by them to the Executive Powers of the different states. This alone is a glaring Evidence of Weakness and Incapacity.

Receiving the Articles of Confederation from the states assembled on November 17, 1777, Clinton submitted them to the legislature on January 16, 1778, and they gained final approval a month later. Although the majority of the members of the legislature of 1778 was decidedly in favor of preserving the rights of the states in full sovereignty and of sustaining the governor and his party, they nevertheless lent their support for the Articles of Confederation. In referring to the adoption of the Articles three years later in 1781, Clinton commented:

> The Articles of Confederation and perpetual union between the thirteen United States are acceded to and formally and finally ratified by all the states. This important event, as it establishes our union, and defeats the first hope of our enemy, cannot but afford the highest satisfaction; and I trust that this state will be as distinguished for the faithful adherence to this great national compact, so essential to the peace and happiness of America, as it has hitherto been for the exertions in the common cause.

Unquestionably, in Clinton's political thought, he adhered to the necessity for national unity and a "great national compact." Only when, however, that national authority became or attempted to become so demanding as to infringe on the liberties of the people would Clinton object and demand that the rights of the states and the people be preserved.

Consequently, Clinton asserted that the legislature of the state should be vigilant and energetic in their duties. He deplored the lack of promptness on the part of the legislators when important business had to be transacted.

> Our legislature were to have met at this place (Poughkeepsie) on the 8th instant, but a sufficient

> number of members have not yet appeared, to proceed
> on business; when they will, God only knows. So little
> attention is paid to the public weal, by the guardians
> of the rights of the people, as to discourage me, more
> than I can well express.

To Clinton, the legislature was the voice of the people, "the guardians of their rights," and the most significant branch of government. In his speeches to the legislature, he consistently states that the legislature should consider the possibility of doing this or doing that. By maintaining the viewpoint that the legislature should govern more and that the governor should govern less, Clinton declared his aversion to the memories of British rule through the channels of the royal governor.

Before considering the manifestations of Clinton's political philosophy as they emerged due to the controversy over the impost problem, it is essential that New York's first governor be recognized as a man that supported and encouraged education. On January 27, 1782, Clinton urged the legislature, and firmly believed, that the government support education, otherwise thoughtfulness and knowledge would cease as pillars of the state. He stated that "it is the particular duty of the government of a free state, where the highest employments are open to citizens of every rank, to endeavor, by the establishment of schools and seminaries, to diffuse that degree of literature which is necessary to the establishment of public trusts."

Indeed, it cannot be said that the first governor of New York State did not understand the importance of education, nor the benefit that learning renders, not only to the progress of the state, but also to the well-being of each individual citizen.

As the first governor of the state, Clinton had fought to make his New York the cornerstone of the new republic. As a war governor, he and his fellow democrats had shown their repudiation of monarchy; monarchy that undeniably meant tyranny, corruption, absentee government, and all that was reprehensible. Republicanism would bring liberty, justice, and civic virtue; opportunity would be opened to all; and government would be based upon the social contract. For George Clinton, his goal from 1776 onward was good government of, by, and for the people. In future conflicts of differing political philosophies, Clinton would not deviate in the pursuit of his goal.

CHAPTER SEVEN

Hamiltonians versus Clintonians

Alexander Hamilton

With the beginning of the decade of the 1780s, an overriding
issue occupied the thoughts of the prominent political minds in the
country – states' rights versus national authority -- whether the united

states were to become a nation or remain a confederation. These views divided political leaders into nationalists and into a group of able and patriotic men who believed that a consolidated national authority was not only unnecessary, but a danger to civil liberty.

Clinton was a member of the latter group, which included such patriots as Patrick Henry, Richard H. Lee, George Mason, James Monroe, Elbridge Gerry, and many others who saw the danger of endowing a national authority with powers that would infringe on the rights of the states. Perhaps it would be more advantageous to comprehend first the political philosophy of Clinton and his fellow statesmen, in order to realize the deep convictions that they espoused in various controversies.

For all intents and purposes, Clinton opposed any extension of the powers of the central government, formed by the Articles of Confederation. Basically, Clinton's political philosophy embodied the following:

> To George Clinton and his Antifederalist friends, a strong centralized government represented the direct antithesis of all that they had fought for in the Revolution. They did not wish to be governed from a faraway capital, taxed by the representatives of other states, and disciplined by standing armies over which they had little or no control. These were just the things that they had objected to under British rule,

and they wanted no more of them. Wars might have to be fought by federal armies, and treaties negotiated by the agents of a distant Congress; but most of the functions of government could be far better and more safely conducted by their own representatives in the city council or state legislature. They wished to be ruled by their own neighbors in their own state, not by the representatives of a dozen other states gathered at a distant capital.

Possibly, if the depression had not occurred during the critical period, 1783-1789, the federal constitution might never have been ratified by the states, for Clinton's political philosophy appealed to a great majority of Americans, who were primarily rural farmers, proprietors, and tradespeople. The sincerity and patriotism of his thought, however, is degraded by federalist-inclined historians, and as previously mentioned, does not receive its true perspective nor its prominent place in the history of our nascent republic.

Although Clinton preferred a federal union instead of consolidation, he became known, not as a federalist, but as an antifederalist. Therefore, it is difficult to perceive of Clinton in 1784, in a speech to the legislature, advocating for a stronger national authority. He stated that, as the legislators must realize, the blessings they were enjoying flowed from the federal union. He recommended attention to "every measure which has a tendency to cement it, and to give that energy to our national councils which may be necessary to the general welfare." However, the real difficulty arose over the differences of opinion on how the federal union was to be cemented, and Clinton seems to have thought that the Articles of Confederation, although a "national compact" forming a "union," was merely a defense alliance of sovereign powers. Thus, it was with this view of the sovereignty of the states in the federal union that Clinton met the problem of the impost.

Hamilton became the leader in New York to collect the most-needed revenue on imports for congress. Although Hamilton had loyal contacts in the New York legislature –- Schuyler and others –- to aid him in collecting the revenue, he nevertheless, in the course of his unrewarding and difficult task, became convinced of the fruitlessness of the ineffectual Articles of Confederation. He objected to the collection of the taxes by state officials, and therefore urged, due to the fact that local collectors failed to provide in many cases the state's quota, that the congress appoint federal officials as collectors.

This proposal by Hamilton met with success only initially, with Clinton having serious doubts after the measure became law in 1781. The legislature of New York on November 21, 1781, approved the collection of the needed and additional revenue from imposts for and by congress, although Clinton, "uniformly in favor of granting an impost to Congress . . . (believed) that, if it were granted in the form recommended, it would prove unproductive, and would lead to the establishment of dangerous principles. I believed that granting the revenue, without giving the power of collection (to Congress) or a control over our state officers, would be the most wise and prudent measure. These are and ever have been my sentiments."

As a military leader, Clinton understood that the acquisition of revenue by the congress was essential, due to the material needs of the men and the war effort itself.

> The indefatigable governor of New York responded to the call with his usual promptitude, and left nothing undone within the scope of his power to put the (impost) quota of the state on the best possible footing . . . The great influence of the governor was exerted with great effect; and to the extraordinary efforts of that patriotic individual, the country is indebted for efficient aid to the main army.

However, he believed that, if the congress and its federal collectors gained control of the impost during the war, they would continue to collect the revenue after peace had been restored. New York's principal port was to be returned to the state in 1783; New York needed revenue badly; and its treasury would welcome the funds from customs. Therefore, Clinton saw a right of the people of the state in jeopardy, and the people of the state whom he represented were not going to be deprived, in a time of frenzy and war, of their right to manage their own affairs in their own state by a distant congress.

Clinton finally had his way in 1783 when the antifederalist-dominated legislature passed a law granting congress the impost but stating that the state must supervise and collect the revenue. Congress refused to accept such an arrangement and demanded Clinton to call the legislature into session to amend their previous law. Clinton refused, thereby giving the Clinton forces a victory for the states-rights philosophy. It must be remembered, however, that Clinton was in favor of a strong national government –- though with limitations –- during the time of war, for such an authority was necessary to provide a united front and a coordinated defense against the enemy. That Clinton advocated the grant of impost revenue to congress can also not be denied:

> I trust there can be no higher Evidence of a sincere Disposition in the State to promote the common interest, than the alacrity with which they passed the law for granting to Congress a duty on Imports, and their present Proffer to accede to any Propositions which may be made for rendering the Union among the States more intimate, and for enabling Congress to draw forth and employ the resources of the whole Empire with the utmost Vigor.

Thus, although Clinton favored a strong national authority during the time of war, he nevertheless felt that congress or any consolidated national authority was to be constantly rebuked when it attempted to encroach on the liberties of the people – even during a time of war.

Clinton's philosophy regarding the impost and the sovereignty of the state caused New York political leaders to divide into Hamiltonians and Clintonians. The party of Clinton had undeniably won a victory over Hamilton and his forces in the struggle over the impost question, or to be more specific, a victory for state's rights. Even though Clinton and Hamilton had found so much to agree upon during the war, they were not at all in agreement by 1786 on the federal issue. And this political rivalry was to continue, eventually to end with a victory for Hamilton in the Poughkeepsie Convention of 1788.

Before the Poughkeepsie Convention was called into session, Clinton was to show himself to be a strong governor, one who must provide the leadership in curbing violence and mob rule in the state. An incident occurred in February of 1787 after the Shays' Rebellion had been suppressed in Massachusetts. With the danger that Shays and his associates would make New York their next center of operations, Clinton ordered the militia to be called out. Within a short period, the militia had dispersed Shays' supporters, therefore assuring New Yorkers that no Shays' Rebellion would occur in their state.

Another indication that the governor would not tolerate disorder in the state was the suppression of the famous doctor's riots in April 1778. In New York City, an aroused mob had broken into a hospital after discovering that an anatomy student was at work on a human specimen. The mob rioted for hours in the street before Clinton called out the troops to restore order.

These two episodes showed that Clinton ruled New York with a firm hand in an era when other states were notorious for governmental laxity. Although Clinton conceived that the functions of government should be held to a minimum, he nonetheless expected government not to tolerate disorder and violence.

At the close of the Revolution, Governor Clinton was at the height of his career. He was one of the great heroes of the war and perhaps the most capable of the war governors. He accepted the high office of governor without abandoning his simplicity of his democratic principles. Known then as a most fervent democrat, Clinton entered the fight over ratification of the Constitution as a man that had remained faithful to the libertarian principles upon which the Revolution had been fought, as the political idol of the masses, and as the most popular man in the state.

CHAPTER EIGHT

Clintonian Democracy and the Constitution

Vice President George Clinton

The census of New York State in 1790 showed that 65,000 people lived in four federalist counties compared to 274,000 people residing in nine antifederalist counties. Of the total number of delegates summoned to pass judgment on the constitution at the Poughkeepsie Convention of 1788, nineteen delegates were federalists and forty-six were antifederalists. Although the state was overwhelmingly opposed to the constitution, many antifederalist delegates, after perceiving that the constitution had been ratified by the required nine states, began to shift their vote for ratification.

Delegates did not want New York to be left out of the union, nor did they cherish the talk of secession by the southern, commercial counties of New York if the constitution was not ratified. However, before the constitution was approved by New York, George Clinton was to become known as the most prominent antifederalist in the country, and Clintonian democracy essentially became synonymous with antifederalism.

The events of the Critical Period in New York State, 1783-1789, leading up to the Poughkeepsie Convention will not generally concern us here. The significant conditions confronting the United States during this period are well-known, but the main tenets of Clintonian democracy, Clinton's political philosophy, are not well-known and, therefore, need to be stressed and emphasized so that the reader may comprehend the basic, overall views of most Americans during the 1780s.

Generally speaking, the most basic conviction in Clinton's political thought was his distaste for any consolidation of national authority that attempted to destroy the liberties of the people. His conception of the state revealed his belief that a government should be "strong and efficient," but that the rights of the state, designed to best protect the liberties of its inhabitants, must predominate in any national republic. Speaking before the convention, after Hamilton had accused Clinton of lamenting over the lack of powers in congress and the defects in the Articles of Confederation, Clinton dramatically stated:

> I declare, solemnly, that I am a friend to a strong and efficient government. But, sir, we may err in this extreme: we may erect a system that will destroy the liberties of the people . . . The people, when wearied with their distresses, will, in the moment of frenzy, be guilty of the most imprudent and desperate measures. Because a strong government was wanted during the late war, does it follow that we should now be obliged to accept of a dangerous one? I ever lamented the feebleness of the Confederation, for this reason, among others, that the experience of its weakness would one day drive the people into an adoption of a constitution dangerous to our liberties. I know the people are too apt to vibrate from one extreme to another. The effects of this disposition are what I wish to guard against.

Liberty and the rights of the common man were frequent cries of George Clinton throughout his public career. He believed that the Revolution had given the United States a government more liberal than any that the world had known. The Revolution had taught the right of resistance to tyranny, and he admonished the people and asked: "For what did you throw off the yoke of Britain and call yourselves independent? Was it . . . to procure new masters . . . and let the rich and insolent alone be your rulers?" To George Clinton's mind, the people were the sovereign rulers of the state. "In democratic republics, the people collectively are considered as the sovereign –- all legislative, judicial, and executive power is inherent in and derived from them." Clinton explained that all people enjoy "freedom, equality, and independence . . . by nature," and that in order to secure these precious principles, the people had "consented to a political power." To Clinton, the fact of the matter was that the new constitution would not render to "all men engaged in political society . . . the preservation of their lives, liberties, and estates."

Naturally, George Clinton was not enthusiastic over the plan for a convention to revise the Articles of Confederation; nor was he jubilant when one of the first decisions of the Philadelphia Convention was that a new government was to be created. As Clinton knew, Hamilton favored a strong, centralized national government, making the states mere administrative units. Even worse, Clinton feared that the new government would, above all, prove dangerous to the liberties of the people, for Hamilton had pointed out that:

> I know there are citizens, who, to gain their own private
> ends, enflame the minds of the well-meaning, tho'
> less intelligent parts of the community, by sating their

vanity with that cordial unfailing specific that all power
is seated in the people. For my part, I am not much
attached to the majority of the multitude, and therefore
waive all pretentions to their countenance. I consider
them in general as ill qualified to judge for themselves
what government will best suit their peculiar situations.

Clinton's views regarding the Philadelphia Convention and the proposed national government are probably best summarized by Robert Yates and John Lansing, two ardent Clintonians, in a letter to Clinton following their withdrawal from the convention in Philadelphia. Their reasons fall into two areas:

> First, they had been authorized to revise the Articles
> of Confederation but not to draft a new constitution
> of government; and second, they could not give their
> approval to the consolidation of the states into one
> national state. A single government, they believed,
> could not administer the vast area of the United States;
> such a government would be expensive to operate;
> and such a government, located far from the homes of
> most of its citizens, would be unresponsive to public
> opinion and dangerous to civil liberties.

Each of these basic planks of Clintonian democracy needs elaboration and each plank needs to be understood so that the "conventional wisdom" of most Americans during this period takes on its proper perspective.

Clinton's political thought evolved around his deep conviction in the sovereignty of the state and did so for very practical reasons. A single government, he believed, could not administer so large a territory as the United States. Emphatically, he made the point that, since the territory of the United States was so extensive, coupled with "the variety of its climates, productions, and commerce, the difference of extent, and number of inhabitants in all, no consolidated republican form of government, with the dissimilitude of interest, morals, and politics," can ever "form a perfect union, establish justice, insure domestic tranquility, promote the general welfare, and secure the blessings of liberty to you and your posterity." And such a national legislature, "composed of interests opposite and dissimilar in their nature, (will) be like a house divided against itself."

Carrying his view of the importance of maintaining state sovereignty even further, he states that:

> In a small territory, maladministration is easily corrected, and designs unfavorable to liberty frustrated and punished. But in large confederacies, the alarm excited by small and gradual encroachments rarely extends to the distant measures, or inspires a general spirit of resistance . . . We find . . . embracing interests as various as their territory is extensive. Their habits,

their productions, their resources, and their political and commercial regulations, are as different as those of any nation upon earth. A general law, therefore, which might be well calculated for Georgia, might operate most disadvantageously and cruelly upon New York.

In other words, Clinton believed that New Yorkers, schooled in a democratic tradition, could have little in common with southerners who were attached to slavery and aristocratic privileges. The liberties of New Yorkers could best be preserved by New Yorkers but could easily be lost if they were risked in the common pool of a single national government.

Indeed, Clinton had a narrow view concerning the centralization of power in the United States. Yet even though he had not adequately analyzed the proposed form of government, he nevertheless saw distinct dangers; dangers that had occupied a top-priority position in his political thought since the outbreak of the Revolution. Arguing for the significance of state legislative power compared to the proposed congress of the United States, Clinton pointed out that:

> The situation of (the state's) agriculture, its commerce, and the system of its resources, will be proportionately more uniform and simple (in comparison to the United States). To a knowledge of these circumstances, therefore, every member of the state legislature will

> be in some degree competent . . . How different will
> be the situation of the general government! The
> body of the legislature will be totally unacquainted
> with all those local circumstances of any particular
> state, which mark the proper object of laws, and
> especially of taxation. A few men, possessed of but a
> very general knowledge of these objects, must alone
> furnish Congress with that information on which they
> are to act . . .

Thus, Clinton, echoing the beliefs of most Americans, revealed his distrust of a distant government and the possible dangers of its power. He saw in the sovereignty of the state the only adequate and sure method of preserving and perpetuating those rights and liberties that he and his fellow countrymen had won as a result of the Revolution. He did not want a new central power to emerge that would only replace the imperial power of Britain, which had only recently been discarded.

George Clinton's political philosophy primarily is embodied in his famous series of "Cato" letters, a series of articles written in rebuttal to the new constitution. However, these letters, published in the *New York Journal*, brought forth an even more famous reply, *The Federalist* letters of Hamilton, Madison, and Jay. Even though the "Cato" letters lacked the scholarly touch of *The Federalist* papers, they nonetheless showed that men were thinking and talking about in 1787.

In the "Cato" letters, Clinton's political philosophy concerning the role of the chief magistrate or president is made clear. He believed that the safety of the people in a republic depended upon the share or proportion that they had in the government; "but experience ought to teach you, that when a man is at the head of an elective government invested with great powers, and interested in his reelection, in what circle appointments will be made; by which means an imperfect aristocracy bordering on monarchy may be established."

> If you will examine, you will perceive that the chief magistrate of this state is your immediate choice, controlled and checked by a just and full representation of the people, divested of the prerogative of influencing war and peace, making treaties, receiving and sending embassies, and commanding standing armies and navies, which belong to the power of the confederation.

Clinton was firmly opposed to the provisions in the new constitution relating to the office of the presidency. He felt that the president, in his "ten-mile square" seat of government, would be possessed with the powers of a monarch. By being in office for four years, the president, Clinton surmised, would obtain patronage and loyalty from many people, thereby endowing himself with the ability to establish a courtly following. However, it must be pointed out that Clinton, as most Americans after the Revolution, feared any such opportunity in their government of establishing a constitutional monarchy. Aristocratic privilege should have no place in the American system of government.

This view of the presidency brings us to another basic tenet of Clinton's thought, and that is, that the people were more tied to the parent, the state, rather than to any large, remote government. He believed that as the circle of authority is enlarged, affection diminishes. Using Montesquieu as his authority, Clinton stressed that a republic must have only a small amount of territory to exist. Governments that were too large tended to break up, just as Maine was ready to break away from Massachusetts, Frankland from North Carolina, and Vermont from New York. Therefore, with such complications of interests, "the science of government will become so intricate and perplexed, and too mysterious for you to understand and observe; and by which you are to be conducted into a monarchy either limited or despotic." Thus, to prevent disintegration, Clinton argues, armies are necessary, and armies destroy liberties.

The struggle against the constitution as George Clinton conceived it, was the old struggle of democracy against privilege. The antifederalists he called "The Friends of the rights of mankind," and the Hamiltonians "the advocates of despotism." The new form of government, Clinton argued, had enormous powers; "the number of representatives are too few, (and) the mode in which they are appointed and their duration will lead to the establishment of an aristocracy;" and "the number of representatives and senators proposed for this vast continent does not equal those of your own state." Clinton believed that most of the representatives, if elected under the new constitution, would be primarily commercial men, and, like Jefferson, Clinton felt that only an agricultural society could remain sound and virtuous, for "the progress of a commercial society begets luxury, the parent of inequality, the foe of virtue, and the enemy to restraint."

In many ways, then, George Clinton espoused the political thought of most Americans, with the struggle over the ratification of the Federal Constitution of 1787 in New York being the culmination of his own political philosophy. From his early years as a legislator, through the war-ridden days of his administration as a war governor, Clinton formulated his philosophy. Throughout these years of his life, Governor Clinton consistently urged that the liberties of the people be protected by all means available to man. Although Clinton lost the fight over ratification of the constitution, he nevertheless was to be a prime mover for the preservation of the liberties of the people – the struggle for the addition of a bill of rights to the constitution. The provisions, then, embodied in the bill of rights were those liberties that Clinton regarded as the most precious possession of all Americans, the preservation of which he dedicated his life.

George Clinton: Vice President of the United States

Conclusion

By tracing George Clinton's actions and career as an assemblyman, as a member of the Second Continental Congress, and as a military leader in New York, one cannot help but come to the realization that, contrary to previous belief, Clinton was not a leader possessed with strong, radical democratic leanings nor a leader for American independence prior to his election as governor of the state of New York. The hostility he showed toward British ministerial policy was a feeling that was shared by most colonists, and like most colonists, Clinton viewed these actions on the part of the mother country as an infringement of the rights, privileges, property, and lives of the king's loyal subjects in America.

The facts reveal that, throughout his career prior to the Declaration of Independence, Clinton desired and hoped that a reconciliation and a redress of grievances could be achieved between Great Britain and the colonies. He viewed the policies of the British government as a radical change in the social and political order in the British Empire, but from all indications, he did not advocate that the remedy lay in the severing of the ties with England. He demanded, fought, and worked for a return to the policy of indirect rule that prevailed between Great Britain and the American colonies prior to 1763.

As we have seen, Clinton did not press for or publicly espouse that the American colonies should be free and independent states. Like many New Yorkers, he understood that the livelihood and prosperity of the colony primarily depended upon trade and cordial relations with the mother country. Consequently, when the hope for reconciliation abated, he vacillated in his view toward independence and simply left the question to the inhabitants of the colony of New York rather than take a strong stand. And when independence was finally declared, he simply accepted and defended the course of action. Clinton's main concern, however, was military defense, and it was due to the respect he acquired as a strong, military leader that he was elected to the governorship of the state of New York.

Clinton's status in the history of the nascent state of New York should be viewed as that of a local, patriotic figure, loyal to the American cause to reconcile past differences with Britain, but hesitant to sever those ties with the mother country that had benefited the colonies for so long a time. In regard to independence, Clinton was not as forceful a leader as men like Thomas Jefferson or John Adams, but militarily, Clinton must be ranked with men like Washington as one of the most respected generals in the Revolution. Clinton's election to the governorship of New York was a tribute to his military leadership during the time of war, and as governor, he continued to exert his leadership, not only as a military commander, but also as a leader devoted to the ideals of the American movement for independence and thereby worthy of being labeled as one of America's Founding Fathers.

Acknowledgments

In 1963, I graduated from Bucknell University in Lewisburg, Pennsylvania, with a Bachelor of Science Degree in Secondary Education. I was a twenty-two-year-old with a plan to eventually teach history either at a public high school or obtain a teaching position on the college level. I was also encouraged and advised to seriously continue my studies and proceed to at least obtain a master's degree, and in the future, consider pursuing a Ph. D. in history. Later on, I envisioned devoting my life to some form of public service, either serving in government or running as a candidate for public office. However, back in the 1960s, Uncle Sam likewise had a plan for me.

When I graduated from Bucknell, I similarly graduated as an infantry officer, a second lieutenant in the United States Army, with a six-year military obligation facing me. A two-year active-duty assignment (deploying to either Germany, Korea, or Vietnam), two years on active reserve, and a two-year period of inactive reserve time. Due to the fact that teaching positions in the 1960s were becoming highly competitive, my professors in the Department of Education recommended that I continue my studies for the next two years, obtain a master's degree during this inactive reserve time, and thereby be highly qualified and competitive in the hiring process that I would face upon returning from my two-year active-duty assignment. Needless to say, it was The Maxwell School of Citizenship and Public Affairs at Syracuse University that welcomed me and proved to be the ideal place for me at this time in my life -- actually, in more ways than one. Since then, I have been extremely grateful and thankful for the opportunity to have studied and worked at this most prestigious and highly respected institution of higher learning. And it was at Maxwell that this book became a reality.

Over the years, I decided to preserve all my research and the bulk of the text of my original master's thesis until the day I would retire from my life as a teacher or public official and then use all my material and additional research to produce a book on this topic. At that time, a thesis was a required component for a master's degree at Maxwell. It had to be equivalent to a doctoral dissertation, an original concept that proved to be a significant contribution to the historical record and based on trustworthy historical evidence and credible research.

In accomplishing this task, I am extremely and especially grateful to so many friends and colleagues. That I have been able to proceed to this point in my life and career, I owe the deepest gratitude and loving affection to my parents, Leo and Anne Kanawada. To have reached this point in my educational career, I wish to remember my former professor of history and an inspiration to me at Bucknell University, Dr. J. Orin Oliphant, and the man who gave me the opportunity to succeed at The Maxwell School, Dr. Warren B. Walsh. Along with Dr. Walsh, I wish to recognize my mentor and friend in the Department of History at Maxwell, Dr. Nelson Manfred Blake and Dr. Richard McKey, both of whom inspired me and piqued my interest in the study of foreign policy, international affairs, and in the politics, political thought, and the life and times in Colonial American history.

Luckily before classes began, I met Dr. Walsh, who was the chairman of the history department at Maxwell. I cite him here because, without him, I never would have had the opportunity to attend Maxwell, to have studied and worked on the graduate level -- or I might add, to eat for the next two years at school without ever opening my wallet! At our first meeting, we immediately hit it off, like a father-son relationship. We seemed to speak the same language, and he thoroughly understood my desire and determination and my personal situation and future military obligation. He expressed his faith in me and encouraged me to attend Maxwell, but it would all be up to me to seize the opportunity.

He wrote to me in June of 1963, "If you wish to enroll next fall in history courses as a non-matriculated student, I'll permit you to register in three graduate courses in history. If you earn B's or better in all three, I'll be in a position to recommend admission for the second semester. This puts it squarely up to you to decide whether to take the risk and the opportunity."

Needless to say, I've always been grateful to him and for him, and also for his parting advice to promptly jog down the hill from Maxwell to see the housemother at the Pi Beta Phi Sorority house where his daughter was a member and the housemother needed waiters for her dining room and dishwashers to man the kitchen. In exchange for your labor, he said, you'll never eat better.

How right he was. No doubt, I landed the most envied job on campus. The housemother selected six of us and, for two years, each of us endured this daily hardship. And I, for some reason, completely suppressed and repressed deep into my unconscious mind any thought of my future military obligation to Uncle Sam.

Before I arrived in Syracuse, I had arranged to rent one of the three rooms at the home of Mom Darrone –- Mrs. Ethel Darrone, a wonderful seventy-year-old grandmother and friend whom I had the pleasure of meeting the previous year. The price was right –- forty dollars a month –- and for that first year at Syracuse, her love and concern for my success and her unselfish hospitality have never been forgotten by me.

In writing this book, I have had the help of a host of people. I am especially thankful for their assistance and encouragement in pursuing my topic. Anyone who studies the early history of our country and the formation of our government owes a debt of gratitude to those who labor with you and for you at the various institutions throughout our country. I wish to extend my special appreciation to those archivists, librarians, assistants, and new friends at the New York State Library in Albany, New York; the New York Public Library in New York City; the National Archives and the Library of Congress in Washington, D.C.; at the Columbia University and Syracuse University libraries; and here in Long Island at the C.W. Post Library of Long Island University, at Hofstra University, and especially at Adelphi University where many hours and years were spent and much of the writing completed.

And, a heartfelt thank you to my publishing consultant at AuthorHouse, Karen Stansberry, and the entire staff on the production and marketing teams. I am indebted to each of you for your concern and professionalism and your exceptional work ethic.

I would be remiss if I did not cite and praise my friend and word processor conversion wizard, Scott Johnson, the manager at Pivar Computing Services in Buffalo Grove, Illinois, in the editing and preparation of the entire manuscript before submission to the production team at AuthorHouse. Many thanks.

Finally, as all historians know, one cannot possibly accomplish any work of this nature without the support of a very special person -- one's wife. To Carol, my wife and best friend for the past fifty plus years, I will always be grateful not only for her preparation of this manuscript, but primarily for her patience, understanding, and love.

Leo V. Kanawada Jr.

Source Notes

NOTE FOR THE READER

For the reader to ascertain or locate the references and page numbers for any specific quote or fact cited in the text of a chapter, a short phrase and its page number is being provided in these source notes.

Each phrase listed has been taken from the end of a sentence or of a paragraph which contains the quoted or factual material that the reader may wish to peruse or reference.

PREFACE

Page

xi "is misleading.": E. Wilder Spaulding, *His Excellency George Clinton* (New York, 1938), 5. Spaulding's interpretation of the status of George Clinton, portraying him as a "thorough-going democrat" and as a "radical" assemblyman in New

York politics, lacks adequate and accurate documentation to substantiate his thesis. Spaulding would have the reader believe that Clinton was a radical leader in New York from 1773 to the introduction of the Declaration of Independence, an advocate of independence, and a governor who was elected by the people due to his strong, democratic leanings. On the contrary, as this book will show, Clinton did little to lead New York, by word or deed, toward independence. He was essentially a local, patriotic figure, echoing the proposals of the Continental Congress, and eventually elected to the governorship as a result of his determined defense of his homeland.

xii   "the office of governor.": George Clinton, *Public Papers of George Clinton, First Governor of New York* (New York and Albany, 1899-1914), 1, 15. Originally, 47 volumes contained the papers of George Clinton, but a fire at the State Library at Albany, New York, in 1911, destroyed most of the volumes, leaving only these 10 volumes pertaining to the period from 1775 to 1789. Evidence about Clinton is, therefore, somewhat difficult to obtain. Nonetheless, an amount sufficient to make a judgment on Clinton and independence still remains.

CHAPTER ONE

Page

2   "of Common Pleas.": Spaulding, *His Excellency George Clinton*, 7.

2   "of the Hudson Valley.": Benjamin Myer Brink, ed., *Olde Ulster* (November 1912) VIII, no. 11, 328.

2   "in Newburgh.": Joseph Bragdon, "Cadwallader Colden, Jr., An Ulster County Tory," *New York State Historical Association Publication*, XXXI (1939), 415.

3   "much hardship and distress.": *Public Papers of George Clinton*, I, 17.

3   "present-day Kingston, New York.": Spaulding, *His Excellency George Clinton*, 15. His father, however, omits all mention of his son in his diary of the expedition. Apparently, Clinton had arrived home "too late to join them." (see Kaminski, 13).

3   "Montreal in 1760.": *Ibid.*

3   "with tongue and pen.": *Ibid.*, 18.

4   "in the province.": *Ibid.*

4   "on August 26, 1765.": *Public Papers of George Clinton*, I, 18.

CHAPTER TWO

Page

6   "important governmental power.": George L. Beer, "British Colonial Policy, 1754-1765," *Political Science Quarterly*, XXII (New York, 1907), 1-48.

6   "over the judiciary.": Carl L. Becker, *The History of Political Parties in the Province of New York, 1760-1776* (Madison, 1909), 6.

6   "rule at home.": *Ibid.*, 5.

6   "on the Hudson to Albany.": *Ibid.*, 8.

7   "supported the landed gentry.": *Ibid.*, 10.

7   "during the colonial period.": *Ibid.*, 11.

8   "with the Assembly.": *Ibid.*, 12.

8   "if their trade would be secure.": *Ibid.*, 51.

8   "discomfort of the Livingstonians.": William Sabine, ed., William Smith's *Memoirs*, 2 volumes (New York, 1958), I, xi.

8   "inslave the colony.": *Ibid.* It is interesting to note that in Smith's *Memoirs* (volume 2, 60n) Clinton is referred to as a "Creature" of William Smith. Even Clinton himself was recorded as having said at that time that "if I am a rebel

Billy Smith made me one. I have been advised by him, have followed his course in whatever I have done and if I am a rebel, I am a rebel of his making." Gilbert D. B. Hasbrouck, "Governor George Clinton," *New York State Historical Association Quarterly,* I (1920), 145. See also Kaminski, 14.

9   "of the Anglican Church.": Thomas Jefferson Wertenbaker, *Father Knickerbocker Rebels* (New York, 1948), 18.

9   "an American Bishopric.": *Ibid.*

9   "in the Assembly.": Becker, *New York*, 60. Philip Livingston.

9   "with the dissenting congregations.": *Ibid.*

9   "and German descent,": Spaulding, *George Clinton*, 32.

10   "derived from their representatives,": Letter from Governor Cadwallader Colden to Secretary Conway, November 9, 1765, in E. B. O'Callaghan, ed., *Documents Relative to the Colonial History of the State of New York* (Albany, 1853-1887), VII, 773.

10   "to the British Constitution.": Sir William Johnson to the Lords of Trade, November 22, 1765, *Documents Relative*, VII, 790.

11   "required by law.": Becker, *New York*, 56.

11   "in payment of debts.": *Ibid.*, 70.

11   "among the poorer classes.": *Ibid.*, 71.

11   "in the colony of New York.": *Ibid.*

12   "not be elected.": *Olde Ulster* (November 1912), VIII, no. 11, 305.

12   "those Northern radicals.": *Ibid.*

12   "were broken off.": *Ibid.*

12   "on October 27, 1768.": Spaulding, *George Clinton*, 22.

13   "on November eighth.": *Ibid.*, 23. In a recent and more extensive biography of George Clinton, based on thorough and detailed research and credible evidence, John Kaminski describes on pages 11-19 Clinton's role and actions devoted toward American independence. At this point in 1768 in Clinton's career, Kaminski writes that, "Although opposed to Parliament's policies embodied in the Quartering Act of 1765 and the Townshend Duties of 1767, Clinton still swore the obligatory oath of allegiance to the Crown and to the royal governor. Assemblyman Clinton was no radical. He hoped to serve his county and assist his party, which still had a small majority in the assembly, in opposing objectional British policy, but he had no thought of independence." Kaminski, 15.

13   "overseers of the poor.": *Journal of the Votes and Proceedings of the General Assembly of the Colony of New York, 1766-1776* (Albany, April 30, 1820), December 31, 1768.

13   "of the royal governor.": Letter from Governor Moore to the Earl of Hillsborough, January 2, 1769, *Documents Relative*, VIII, 144.

14   "among their Livingstonian friends.": George W. Schuyler, *Colonial New York* (New York, 1885), 262.

14   "for better roads for Ulster,": *Journal of the Legislative Council* (Albany, 1861), December 8, 1769.

14   "at Ulster vendues.": *Journal of the Assembly*, May 20, 1769.

14   "discrimination of various kinds.": *Journal of the Assembly*, 12, 1770. January 9, 24, 25, 1770.

14   "public highways,": *Journal of the Legislative Council*, January 12, 1770.

14   "inns and taverns,": *Ibid.*, January 24, 1770.

14   "beef repackers,": *Ibid.*, January 29, 1771.

14   "of spiritous liquors at Vendues,": *Ibid.*, January 23, 1772.

14   "beagles in Ulster County.": *Ibid.*, February 11, 1773.

15   "in the Revolution.": Spaulding, *George Clinton*, 31. Lee, *George Clinton: Master Builder of the Empire State*, 4. Lee acknowledges that his book on Clinton is a "condensed biography" and confesses that the "biographies by Kaminski and Spaulding inspired me to continue presenting Clinton's

accomplishments with hopes that his contributions are appreciated by the widest readership possible. In this endeavor I have tried to extract for the reader the most salient and interesting material from their writings." Lee, xviii.

15   "and Ten Broeck.": Schuyler, *Colonial New York*, I, 386.

15   "of the mercantile interest." Henry C. Van Schaack, ed., *Life of Peter Van Schaack* (New York, 1842), 10-11.

16   "such a question should not be put.": Sabine, ed., Smith's *Memoirs*, I, 63.

16   "to the elector and elected.": *Ibid.*, 64.

16   "of their constituencies.": *Journal of the Assembly*, April 12, 21, 1769.

16   "and Clinton and Schuyler,": *Ibid.*

17   "that signed the agreement.": Becker, *New York*, 84.

17   "the proper supplies (for the troops);": Governor Moore to Hillsborough, July 11, 1769, *Documents Relative*, VIII, 175.

17   "for ten pounds.": Colden to Hillsborough, July 11, 1769, *Documents Relative*, VIII, 175.

17   "bills of credit,": Becker, *New York*, 77.

17   "our most serious consideration.": Sabine, ed., Smith's *Memoirs*, I, 62.

17   "bills of credit, then pending, became law,": *Journal of the Assembly*, December 15, 1769.

18   "of the City and Colony of New York.": Becker, *New York*, 80.

18   "his influence in the Assembly.": Ibid; See also Sabine, ed., Smith's *Memoirs*, I, 67.

18   "of any summary proceedings.": Spaulding, *George Clinton*, 29.

18   "by any overstrained authority.": *Ibid.*

19   "Schuyler voted no to the motion.": Sabine, ed., Smith's *Memoirs*, I, 72.

19   "Merchandizes imported into the colony.": *Journal of the Legislative Council*, January 18, 1772.

20   "one of the delinquents.": Spaulding, *George Clinton*, 34-35.

CHAPTER THREE

Page

23   "throughout the colony.": Becker, *New York*, 96.

23   "vote against the appropriation.": *Journal of the Assembly*, February 18, 1773.

23   "proprietor's rent and taxation.": Becker, *New York*, 78.

23   "for the British troops.": *Journal of the Assembly*, February 19, 1773.

23   "additional L 800 for the troops.": *Ibid.*, March 5, 1773. The vote was 11-10.

23   "acceptable to the colonists.": Becker, *New York*, 95.

23   "advocated as unconstitutional.": *Ibid.*, 104.

24   "to pay an unconstitutional tax.": *New York Journal*, October 14, 1773.

24   "government by revenue laws.": Sabine, ed., Smith's *Memoirs*, I, 156.

24   "importation of tea.": Becker, *New York*, 111.

25   "and George Clinton.": *Journal of the Assembly*, January 20, 1774.

25   "in future contests.": Becker, *New York*, 111.

25   "from the Manor of Livingston,": *Journal of the Assembly*, January 26, 1774.

25   "of the General Assembly.": *Journal of the Assembly*, February 21, 1774.

26   "on this particular issue.": Sabine, ed., Smith's *Memoirs*, I 176.

26   "British troops in the colony.": *Journal of the Assembly*, January 25, 1774; February 8, 1774.

26   "to his home at New Windsor.": Spaulding, *George Clinton*, 36.

26   "acquired in the Course of it.": Sabine, ed., Smith's *Memoirs*, I, 179.

27   "shall compel them to do it.": Van Schaack, *Life of Peter Van Schaack*, 28.

27   "to the radical policy of non-importation." Becker, *New York*, 113.

28   "of the people of New York.": *Ibid.*, 115.

28   "the policies of the British government.": *Ibid.*, 119.

28   "and county of New York.": *Ibid.*, 140.

28   "sending delegates to Philadelphia.": *New York Mercury*, September 5, 1774.

29   "to advocate at the Congress.": Becker, *New York*, 135.

29   "by the Citizens Of New York City),": Thomas Jones, *History of New York During the Revolutionary War* (New York, 1879), I, 469.

29   "and confiscation of property.": Becker, *New York*, 154.

29   "Congress under the same conditions.": *Ibid.*, 157.

30   "the alleged tyranny of Parliament.": *Ibid.*, 160.

30   "of the extra-legal movement.": *Ibid.*, 161.

30   "in the fall of 1774.": Spaulding, *George Clinton*, 37.

30   "appoint committees to enforce it.": Becker, *New York*, 171.

30   "threatened with tar and feathers.": *Ibid.*

31   "the dominant de Lanceyite-loyalist faction.": *Journal of the Assembly*, January 26, 1775.

31   "this session of the Assembly.": *Ibid.* This group included Schuyler, Clinton, Boerum, P. Livingston, DeWitt, Woodhull, B. Seaman, Ten Broeck, and Van Cortlandt.

31   "to the First Continental Congress,": *Journal of the Assembly*, February 17, 1775.

31   "the non-intercourse agreement,": *Ibid.*, February 21, 1775.

31   "to the Second Continental Congress,": *Ibid.*, February 23, 1775.

31   "a vote of seventeen to nine.": *Ibid.*

32   "and the sooner the better.": Jones, *History of New York*, II, 328.

32   "than to desert Great Britain.": Becker, *New York*, 176.

32   "assembly did not dare recognize.": *Ibid.*, 178.

32   "and his were often refused.": Sabine, ed., Smith's *Memoirs*, I, 213.

32   "on the matter of grievances.": Becker, *New York*, 178.

33   "Rapalje, Kissam, and Nicoll.": *Journal of the Assembly*, January 31, 1775. To view the basic substance of the report on grievances, see Becker, *New York*, 177. Note that no mention of independence is listed.

33   "in America without their consent.": *Ibid.*, March 3, 24, 1775.

33   "of His Majesty's dominions." *Ibid.*, March 3, 1775.

34   "of your Majesty's American subjects.": *Ibid.*, March 24, 1775.

34   "affected the colony of New York.": *Ibid.*, March 3, 1775.

34   "to prevent our obtaining redress.": *Ibid.*, March 24, 1775.

34   "their fellow subjects in Britain.": *Ibid.*

34   "the Liberty Boys in N. England.": Sabine, ed., Smith's *Memoirs*, I, 215.

35   "in Quebec, were also grievances.": *Journal of the Assembly*, March 3, 1775.

35   "independent of the people.": *Ibid.*, March 24, 1775.

35   "the maxims of sound philosophy,": *Ibid.*

35   "upon all the various sects.": Spaulding, *George Clinton*, 39.

35   "by a desire for independence.": *Journal of the Assembly*, March 24, 1775.

35   "in the British Parliament.": *Ibid.*

36   "in the Regulation of Commerce.": *Ibid.*

36   "Assembly adjourned on April 3, 1775.": Becker, *New York*, 177.

36   "composed of both factions.": *Ibid.*

36   "New York Provincial Convention.": *Ibid.*, 188.

CHAPTER FOUR

Page

37   "in general Congress.": Becker, *New York*, 179.

38   "in New York City on April 20, 1775.": *New York Mercury*, March 20, 1775.

38   "the path of loyalism.": Becker, *New York*, 187.

38   "and George Clinton.": *Public Papers of George Clinton*, I, 55.

38   "and finally tyranny.": Bragdon, "Cadwallader Colden, Jr.: An Ulster County Tory," XXXI, 416.

39   "in April of 1775.": *Olde Ulster*, II, no. 10, 303.

39   "and Liberties of America.": *Ibid.*

39   "and her Amer. Colonies.": *Ibid.*

39   "for reconciliation with Great Britain.": Allan Nevins, *The American States During and After the Revolution, 1775-1789* (New York, 1924), 15.

39   "in the Second Continental Congress.": Becker, *New York*, 192.

40   "to the cause of the Congress.": Sabine, ed., Smith's *Memoirs*, I, xi.

40   "between Great Britain and the Colonies.": *Journals of the Proceedings of Congress Held at Philadelphia*, (Philadelphia, 1777), 75.

40   "armed citizens paraded in the streets.": Becker, *New York*, 193.

40   "of the Second Continental Congress.": *Ibid.*, 199.

40   "of conducting a war,": *Journals of the Continental Congress* (1777), 75.

41   "and ammunition and supplies secured.": Becker, *New York*, 217.

41   "of the army of the United Colonies.": Worthington C. Ford, ed., *Journals of the Continental Congress* (Washington, 1904), II, 96.

41   "or right they could never effect.": *Ibid.*, II, 128.

42   "for the Establishment of ... tranquility.": Sabine, ed., Smith's *Memoirs*, I, 233.

42   "rather than independence.": *Public Papers of George Clinton*, I, 212.

43   "and superintend military affairs.": *Olde Ulster*, II, no. 3, 273.

43   "in New York during the Revolution.": *Public Papers of George Clinton*, I, 196.

43   "supply everything for them.": *Ibid.*, I, 198.

43   "induce better men to enlist.": *Ibid.*, I, 206.

43   "for our much injured Country,": *Ibid.*, I, 209.

43   "for the Cause of Liberty.": *Ibid.*, I, 212.

44   "until December of 1775.": *Ibid.*, I, 214. In Clinton's public papers, no correspondence was transmitted by Clinton from August 1775, until January 1776.

44   "risen from the grave.": *Ibid.*

44   "of this vain and anxious Life.": *Ibid.*, I, 215.

44   "in a state of rebellion.": Becker, *New York*, 222.

44   "some scheme of reconciliation.": *Ibid.*

44   "and declare independence.": *Ibid.*, 229.

44   "of the non-intercourse policy.": *Ibid.*, 254.

45   "in the colony of New York.": *Ibid.*

45   "a revival of prosperity.": O'Callaghan, ed., *Documents Relative*, VIII, 666.

45   "to pardon repentant rebels.": Becker, *New York*, 254.

45   "being reduced to the State of 1763.": Sabine, ed., Smith's *Memoirs*, II, 417.

45   "a brigadier general in the militia.": *Public Papers of George Clinton*, I, 98.

46   "in the Northern End of Ulster County.": *Ibid.*, I, 217.

46   "of the New York Highlands.": *Ibid.*, I, 98.

46   "of the revolutionists themselves.": Becker, *New York*, 256.

46   "into the arena of war.": *Ibid.*

47   "reasonably "oligarchic" or broadly democratic.": *Ibid.*

47   "a delegate to the Continental Congress.": *Ibid.*, 259.

47   "could drag Great Britain after him.": Sabine, ed., Smith's *Memoirs*, II, 417. Thomas Jones stated that Clinton expressed similar sentiments in Philadelphia in a speech when he "went so far as to wish a poniard (a dagger) in the heart of George

the tyrant of Britain and would gladly contribute towards a handsome reward to any person who would perform so religious, so glorious, and so patriotic an act." However, no mention of independence was reported in Clinton's remarks. Thomas Jones, *History of New York During the Revolutionary War*, II, 328. See also Kaminski, 18.

47 "when he was going to Philad.": *Ibid.*

47 "He (Clinton) said Jay was right.": *Ibid.*

47 "free and independent states.": Ford, *Journals of the Continental Congress*, V, 425.

48 "never leave their chairs.": Rutledge to Jay, June 29, 1776: *Correspondence and Public Papers of John Jay*, I, 67. See also Becker, 271.

48 "a new government and to independence.": Becker, *New York*, 271.

48 "for a declaration of independence.": *Ibid.*, 271-274.

CHAPTER FIVE

Page

51 "loyalty to the new-born state.": Becker, *New York*, 274.

51 "prominent political status in New York.": Wertenbaker, 82.

52   "democratic at the bottom.": Becker, *New York*, 275.

52   "Dutchess, Ulster, Orange, and Westchester.": *Public Papers of George Clinton*, I, 98.

53   "to appoint officials would be limited.": Spaulding, *George Clinton*, 86.

53   "in the apportionment of representatives.": Nevins, 15.

53   "centralized and measurably aristocratic.": Becker, *New York,* 276.

53   "would have cracked the cord'.": *Ibid.*

53   "of the courthouse at Kingston.": Alexander C. Flick, *The American Revolution in New York: Its Political, Social, and Economic Significance* (Albany, 1926), 85.

54   "John Morin Scott, and George Clinton.": Raymond Smith, *Political and Governmental History of the State of New York* (Syracuse, 1922), I, 57.

54   "held little appeal to the moderates.": Spaulding, *George Clinton,* 90.

54   "to vote at the Forts.": Sabine, ed., Smith's *Memoirs*, II, 159.

55   "they have voted for the latter.": *Ibid.*, II, 170.

55   "to the New Model (state government).": *Ibid.*

55   "Schuyler 1199, and Clinton 1828.": Spaulding, *George Clinton*, 92.

55   "James (Clinton) is the oldest General.": Sabine, ed., Smith's *Memoirs*, II, 172.

55   "who amassed 1098 votes.": Spaulding, *George Clinton*, 93.

55   "to Pierre Van Cortlandt.": Smith, *Political and Governmental History,* I, 60.

56   "few men are his Superiors.": Spaulding, *George Clinton*, 82.

56   "support, countenance, and comfort.": *Public Papers of John Jay*, I, 147.

56   "as it at present experiences.": John C. Fitzpatrick, ed., *Writings of George Washington*, 39 volumes, (Washington, D. C., 1931-1944), IX, 15. As one of Clinton's prominent biographers, Spaulding likewise echoed Washington's portrayal of Clinton's character and the reasons for Clinton's success as a candidate for the governorship. "Most important of all, he had contributed more to the waging of the war than any other general officer from New York with the possible exception of Philip Schuyler. His intense devotion to the American cause, his long months of service in the field at the expense of his health and personal interests, his rugged straight-forward qualities, his preeminent common sense, his energy –– these factors and others had won Washington's

confidence and the admiration of thousands of New Yorkers."
Spaulding, *George Clinton*, 59.

57   "to the floundering state of finances.": Charles Lincoln, ed., *Messages from the Governors* (Albany, 1909), II, 9.

57   "to the defense of the Highlands,": *Olde Ulster*, II, no. 3, 274.

57   "to risk everything for Independency.": Sabine, ed., Smith's *Memoirs*, II, 379.

57   "and would (if necessary) die in the cause.": *Ibid.*, II, 417.

CHAPTER SIX

Page

60   "so much to support.": Charles Lincoln, ed., *Messages From the Governors* (Albany, 1909), II, 9. See also Kaminski, 96-106.

60   "guardians of their rights. " : *Ibid.*, II, 10.

60   "placed in their persons.":

61   "crusade against the Tories.": Spaulding, *George Clinton*, 110. See also Kaminski, 77-81.

61   "disenfranchised in 1784.": *Ibid.*

61   "to a damned Tory.": *Ibid.*

61   "was moderate and fair.": Flick, *The American Revolution in New York*, 225.

62   "of Weakness and Incapacity.": Clinton, *Public Papers*, II, 865.

62   "final approval a month later.": Spaulding, *George Clinton*, 114.

62   "the governor and his party,": Isaac Q. Leake, *Memoir of the Life and Times of General John Lamb* (Albany: J. Munsell, 1857), 303.

63   "in the common cause.": Lincoln, *Messages From the Governors*, II, 127.

64   "I can well express.": Leake, *Memoir of John Lamb*, 216.

64   "establishment of public trusts.": *The American States*, 467. See also Kaminski, 5-6, 266.

65   "and for the people.": Spaulding, *George Clinton*, 141.

CHAPTER SEVEN

Page

68   "danger to civil liberty.": Raymond Smith, *Political and Governmental History*, 96.

69   "gathered at a distant capital.": Spaulding, *George Clinton*, 167.

70   "to the general welfare.": Lincoln, *Messages From the Governors*, II, 196.

70   "defense alliance of sovereign powers.": Smith, *Political and Governmental History,* 96

70   "federal officials as collectors.": Nathan Schachner, *Alexander Hamilton* (New York and London: Appleton-Century Company, Inc., 1946), 147. See also Kaminski, 48.

71   "ever have been my sentiments.": Jonathan Elliot, ed., *Debates in the Several State Conventions on the Adoption of the Federal Constitution* (Philadelphia, 1891), II, 359.

71   "efficient aid to the main army.": Leake, *of John Lamb*, 288. See also Kaminski, 53-54.

71   "welcome the funds from customs.": Spaulding, *George Clinton*, 168. See also Kaminski, 126-129, 178-189, 267.

72   "and collect the revenue.": Smith, *Political and Governmental History,* 96. See also Kaminski, 89-96.

72   "with the utmost Vigor.": Clinton, *Public Papers*, VII, 521.

73   "on the federal issue.": Spaulding, *George Clinton*, 170.

73   "would occur in their state.": *Ibid.*, 164.

73   "the troops to restore order.": *Ibid.*

74   "capable of the war governors.": *Ibid.*, 158

CHAPTER EIGHT

Page

75 "in nine antifederalist counties.": E. Wilder Spaulding, *New York in the Critical Period, 1783-1789* (New York: Columbia University Press, 1932), 201.

76 "forty-six were antifederalists.": *Ibid.*

76 "constitution was not ratified.": *Ibid.*, 255.

77 "I wish to guard against." Elliot, *Debates*, II, 359.

78 "insolent alone be your rulers?": Paul L. Ford., ed., *Essays on the Constitution of the United States* (Brooklyn: Historical Printing Club, 1892), 251.

78 "and derived from them.": *Ibid.*

78 "consented to a political power." *Ibid.*, 255.

78 "their lives, liberties, and estates.": *Ibid.*

78 "mere administrative units.": Spaulding, *George Clinton*, 171. See also Kaminski, 122-131.

79 "suit their peculiar situations.": Ford, *Essays on the Constitution*, 287.

79 "dangerous to civil liberties.": Spaulding, *George Clinton*, 172.

80   "a house divided against itself.": Ford, *Essays on the Constitution*, 258.

81   "cruelly upon New York.": Elliot, *Debates*, 262.

81   "a single national government.": Spaulding, *George Clinton*, 174.

82   "on which they are to act . . .": Elliot, *Debates*, 261. See also Kaminski, 140-148, 163-166.

82   "talking about in 1787.": Spaulding, *George Clinton*, 173. See also Kaminski, 131-135; Lee, *George Clinton*, xiii-xv, 29-30.

83   "may be established.": Ford, *Essays on the Constitution*, 264.

83   "power of the confederation.": *Ibid.*

83   "the powers of a monarch.": *Ibid.*, 262.

84   "and Vermont from New York.": *Ibid.*, 256.

84   "either limited or despotic.": *Ibid.*, 257.

84   "the advocates of despotism.": Spaulding, *George Clinton*, 176.

85   "those of your own state.": Ford, *Essays on the Constitution*, 269.

85   "and the enemy to restraint.": *Ibid.*, 266. See also Kaminski, 197-201.

Bibliography

A NOTE ON SOURCES

In order to examine the life of George Clinton and his actions and thoughts pertaining to American Independence, I have relied heavily on several primary works. Some 37 volumes of George Clinton's papers were destroyed in a fire at the State Library at Albany, New York, in 1911, thereby making it somewhat difficult to obtain his personal reactions toward the events leading up to and including the separation of the American colonies from Great Britain. Nevertheless, ample evidence remained so that an accurate judgment on Clinton and independence could be achieved.

PRIMARY SOURCES

Possibly the most beneficial work for a more than satisfactory account of the thoughts and actions of George Clinton as a member of the New York Assembly is William H. W. Sabine, ed., William

Smith's *Memoirs* (2 volumes, New York, 1958). Of all of Clinton's contemporaries and friends during the years before the Revolution, only Smith records Clinton's career in some detail, clearly expressing Clinton's role as a prominent member in the Livingston faction and his thoughts concerning independence as a loyal patriot. The *Public Papers of George Clinton* (10 volumes, New York and Albany, 1899-1914) provide a valuable military history of the Revolution and Clinton's politics as governor, but unfortunately, they do not reveal Clinton's earlier years except for a short, accurate biographical sketch in volume one.

Party politics in New York and Clinton's political career as a member of the Livingston faction in the Assembly required a careful examination in order to give coherence to Clinton's evolution as an outspoken, but local, patriotic figure in New York before the Revolution. In attempting the political analysis of Clinton's career, the *Journals of the Votes and Proceedings of the General Assembly of the Colony of New York, 1766-1776* (Albany, 1820), and the *Journal of the Legislative Council of the Colony of New York, 1691-1775* (Albany, 1861), proved to be the most accurate and beneficial documentation available. In the *Journal of the Proceedings of Congress Held at Philadelphia, 1774-1776* (Philadelphia, 1777), in the work of Worthington C. Ford, ed., *Journals of the Continental Congress* (Washington, D.C., 1904), and in the *Journal of the Provincial Congress, Provincial Convention, Committee on Safety, and Council of Safety of the State of New York* (2 volumes, Albany,

1842), the record shows that Clinton spoke very little -- and the same is true of Clinton in the Second Continental Congress.

To better understand and to trace the views of New Yorkers concerning colonial resistance toward the policies of the British government, I consulted several newspapers and volumes of documents that were particularly good in indicating the colony's position. References to George Clinton are negligible in John Holt's radical, anti-British paper, the *New York Journal* (New York, 1766-1776) and, in Hugh Gaines' *New York Gazette and Weekly Mercury* (New York, 1768-1783), but their value as a measure to ascertain colonial sentiments toward Great Britain is most useful. Likewise, the work of Edmund O'Callaghan, ed., *Documents Relative to the Colonial History of the State of New York* (10 volumes, Albany, 1853-1887), provides an excellent view of the reactions and attitudes of various officials in the colony.

When hostilities broke out in the colonies in the spring of 1775, New York politics showed a realignment of the inhabitants into loyalist and patriot parties. During this period, Clinton's status was that of a local, patriotic figure, but by no means a prominent patriot leader in the colonies or a radical leader in New York. The writings and memoirs of the following men discuss the status and actions of Clinton as a patriotic figure from 1775 until his election as governor, proving most helpful, along with Smith's *Memoirs*, in determining Clinton's attitude toward American independence; loyalist Thomas Jones, *History of New York During the Revolutionary War* (2 volumes, New York, 1879);

Paul Leicester Ford, ed., *The Writings of Thomas Jefferson* (New York, 1892); W. W. Campbell, *Life and Writings of DeWitt Clinton* (New York, 1849); John Fitzpatrick, ed., *Writings of George Washington* (39 volumes, Washington, D.C., 1931-1944); Henry Johnston, ed., *The Correspondence and Public Papers of John Jay* (volumes 1 and 2, New York, 1890); and Isaac Leake, *Memoir of the Life and Times of General John Lamb* (Albany, 1857). An excellent source on the public utterances of the colonial governors of New York and of George Clinton's tenure as governor of the state of New York has been compiled by Charles Lincoln, ed., *Messages from the Governors* (Volumes 1 and 2, Albany, 1909).

SECONDARY SOURCES

The major work on the life of George Clinton is E. Wilder Spaulding's biography, *His Excellency George Clinton* (New York, 1938), that advances an inaccurate view, in my opinion, that Clinton was a "thorough-going democrat," a "radical" leader in New York favoring independence, and a governor elected by the people due to his strong, democratic leanings. After examining and reading the sources in Spaulding's bibliography, I believe that, had he consulted William Smith's *Memoirs*, his interpretation of Clinton and his attitudes and actions pertaining to American independence would have somewhat resembled the thoughts in this book. A short biographical sketch, inaccurate at some points, of George Clinton can also be found in an article by John S. Jenkins, "Governor George Clinton," *Lives of the Governors of the State of New York* (Auburn, 1852).

Probably the most primary secondary source, on which I have relied heavily, for any study of New York colonial politics prior to the Revolution is Carl Becker's excellent work, *History of Political Parties in the Province of New York, 1760-1776* (Madison, 1909). This study, stressing the economic and social divisions in New York, examines a contest not only about home rule but also concerning who should rule at home.

In addition to the work by Carl Becker, one should also consult the studies of Bernard Mason, *The Road To Independence: The Revolutionary Movement in New York, 1773-1777* (Lexington, 1966), and Alfred F. Young, *The Democratic Republicans of New York: The Origins, 1763-1797* (Chapel Hill, 1967), in order to explore the view that Clinton's politics and actions were more in line with the moderate factions in New York. To obtain a contrasting viewpoint of Clinton similar to Spaulding's conclusion that Clinton was a radical and a leader of this faction in New York, see the recent works by John P. Kaminski, *George Clinton: Yeoman Politician of the New Republic* (Madison, 1993), John K. Lee, *George Clinton: Master Builder of the Empire State* (Syracuse, 2010), and Jerome Mushkat, *George Clinton: New York Governor During Revolutionary Times* (Charlotteville, 1974).

To ascertain Clinton's role and status in New York politics, George Schuyler's *Colonial New York* (2 volumes, New York, 1885) provides an adequate study of the Schuyler family, including Philip Schuyler's relationship with George Clinton. A source that is useful for a general knowledge of the governmental history of the province and State of New York is Raymond B. Smith's *Political and Governmental History of the State of New York* (Volume 1, Syracuse, 1922). Alexander Flick's study of the significance of the American Revolution, *The American Revolution in New York: Its Political, Social, and Economic Significance* (Albany, 1926), and Thomas Jefferson Wertenbaker's *Father Knickerbocker Rebels* (New York, 1948), emphasizes the conflicts between loyalist and patriot parties in New York, and proved helpful in relating Clinton's attitudes toward the patriot movement and independence.

The reader who wishes to gain a more than adequate knowledge of the political, social, and economic relationship between New York and the other American colonies during the Revolutionary period will find the following works extremely beneficial: Allan Nevins, *The American States During and After the Revolution, 1775-1789* (New York, 1924); J. Franklin Jameson, *The American Revolution Considered as a Social Movement* (Princeton, 1926); Vernon L. Parrington, *Main Currents in American Thought: The Colonial Mind, 1620-1800* (New York, 1927); Arthur Meier Schlesinger, *New Viewpoints in American History* (New York, 1925); and C. H. Van Tyne, *The Cause of the War for Independence* (Boston, 1922).

Although the following two works, John Fiske's *The Critical Period of American History, 1782-1789* (Boston and New York, 1897), and E. Wilder Spaulding's *New York in the Critical Period, 1783-1789* (New York, 1932), deal mainly with the Critical Period in American history, they nonetheless provide sufficient information about George Clinton's election to the governorship of New York and his first term of office. Andrew Cunningham McLaughlin's classic study, *The Confederation and The Constitution* (New York, 1905), is also useful for an understanding of conditions that prevailed in New York after the Revolution.

In attempting to form an opinion of Clinton's attitude toward the conflicts between Great Britain and the American colonies, and his views toward independence, I found the work of Henry Van Schaack, *Life of Peter Van Schaack* (New York, 1842), a most valuable aid for comprehending the sentiments of the colonists, both loyalist and patriot, toward the extra-legal movement. The work of John C. Hamilton, *The Life of Alexander Hamilton* (Volume 2, New York, 1840), Nathan Schachner, *Alexander Hamilton* (New York and London, 1946), and Jared Sparks, *The Life of Gouverneur Morris* (Boston, 1832), also provide pertinent material on the extra-legal movement in New York. For a most adequate discussion of the views of the outstanding loyalists in the colonies, William Nelson's *The American Tory* (Oxford, 1961), is available.

George L. Beer's study, "British Colonial Policy", *Political Science Quarterly*, Volume XXII (New York, 1907), pp. 1-48, is useful for a brief account of the organization and colonial policy of the British Empire.

For any understanding of George Clinton prior to the Revolution and his thoughts toward independence, the reader will find it necessary to examine the political, social, and economic climate that existed in Ulster County. I have found that the work of Benjamin

Brink, ed., *Olde Ulster* (Kingston, 1906), and Joseph Bragdon's article, "Cadwallader Colden, II -- An Ulster County Tory," *New York Historical Association Publication*, Volume XXXI (New York, 1933), pp. 411-421, give perhaps the best insight into Clinton's relation to the inhabitants of Ulster County, and his views as well as the Ulsterite view toward independence.

BOOKS, PUBLIC AND PRIVATE PAPERS

Since a number of various items listed in this bibliography do not include a complete or detailed citation –- particularly the journals and diaries or an individual's public or private papers and correspondence –- the internet should be consulted for their availability and present-day locations. Suffice it to say, however, that the bulk of these items and books and sources that I have used and consulted over the years in writing this book still reside in either the Library of Congress, the National Archives, the New York Public Library, or in the State Library in Albany, New York, and/or can be found and are listed –- rather than duplicating so many of the books here -- in the extensive and detailed bibliographies and source notes compiled in the biographies written by Spaulding and Kaminski.

Bowers, Claude G. *Jefferson and Hamilton: The Struggle for Democracy in America*. Boston: Houghton, Mifflin, and Company, 1925.

Boyd, Julian P., et al, editor. *The Papers of Thomas Jefferson*. Princeton, 1950.

Burnett, Edmund C., editor. *Letters of Members of the Continental Congress.* 8 volumes (Washington, D.C., 1921-1936).

Champagne, Roger J. *Alexander McDougall and the American Revolution in New York.* Schenectady, New York, 1975.

Clinton, DeWitt. *The Papers of DeWitt Clinton.* Columbia University.

Dawson, Henry B., editor. *The Federalist.* Volume 1. Morrisania, New York: H. O. Houghton, 1864.

DePauw, Linda Grant. *The Eleventh Pillar: New York State and the Federal Constitution.* Ithaca, New York, 1966.

Elliot, Jonathan. *Debates in the Several State Conventions on the Adoption of the Federal Constitution.* Volume 2. Philadelphia: J.B. Lippincott Company, 1891.

Farrand, Max. *Chronicles of America: The Fathers of the Constitution.* New Haven: Yale University Press, 1921.

Flexner, James Thomas. *Washington: The Indispensable Man.* Boston: Little, Brown, and Company, 1969.

Flick, Alexander C. *Loyalism in New York During the American Revolution.* New York: Columbia University Press, 1901.

Ford, Paul Leicester, editor. *The Writings of Thomas Jefferson.* New York, 1892.

Gerlach, Don R. *Proud Patriot: Philip Schuyler and the War of Independence, 1775-1783.* Syracuse, 1987.

Hammond, Jabez. *The History of Political Parties in the State of New York.* 1842.

Hasbrouck, Gilbert D. B. "Governor George Clinton", *New York State Historical Association Quarterly.* Volume 1. 1920.

Livingston Papers, Robert R. New York Historical Society.

McCullough, David. *John Adams.* New York: Simon and Schuster, 2001.

McCullough, David. *1776.* New York: Simon and Schuster, 2005.

Morris, Anne Cary, editor. *The Diary and Letters of Gouverneur Morris.* 2 volumes. New York, 1888.

Morris, Gouverneur. *An Oration in Honor of the Memory of George Clinton.* New York, 1812.

Morris, Richard B., editor. *John Jay: The Making of a Revolutionary, Unpublished Papers, 1745-1780.* New York, 1975.

Morris, Richard B. *The American Revolution: A Short History.* New York: D. Van Nostrand Company, Inc., 1955.

Randall, Willard Sterne. *Thomas Jefferson: A Life.* New York: Henry Holt and Company, 1993.

Schechter, Stephen L., and Richard B. Bernstein, editors. *New York and the Union: Contributions to the American Constitutional Experience.* Albany, 1990.

Schecter, Barnet. *The Battle for New York.* New York: Walker and Company, 2002.

Smith, Paul H., et.al., editors. *Letters of Delegates to Congress, 1774-1789.* Washington, D.C., 1976.

Stone, William L. "George Clinton," *Magazine of American History,* June 1879.

Strayer, Joseph R. *The Delegate from New York.* Princeton Princeton University Press, 1939.

Syrett, Harold C., editor. *The Papers of Alexander Hamilton.* 27 volumes. New York, 1961-1987.

Upton, L.F.S. *The Loyal Whig: William Smith of New York and Quebec.* Toronto: University of Toronto Press, 1969.

Index

clerk of Ulster County court of
common pleas, 3, 4

commissioned brigadier general,
42, 45, 46

appointed to Committee of
Correspondence (1774), 25

appointed to Committee of
Grievances (1775), 33, 34,
35, 36, 42, 43, 47

delegate to New York General
Assembly, 4, 9

delegate to Second Continental
Congress (1775), 38, 39

Doctor's Riots, 73

early occupations, 3

education of, 2, 3, 64, 65

federal impost, 64, 70, 71, 72, 73

first inaugural address, 57

governor, elected, xi, 52, 55,
56, 57

legal studies of, 3

loyalists, 29, 30, 32, 38, 43, 46,
51, 61

marriage of, 14

McDougall affair, 18, 19

military and funds for British
troops, 11, 16, 17, 19, 22,
23, 25, 26, 38

military general, 54, 55

paper money, 11, 59, 60

Provincial Convention (1775), 36,
38, 39, 40

public education, 2, 3, 64, 65

religion, 2

Republicanism, 65

rights of the people, 63, 64, 76,
77, 78

severe illness, 43, 44, 114

Shays' Rebellion, 73

stable currency, 60

state constitution, 52

states' rights, 61, 62, 63, 64,
67, 68, 69, 72, 73, 76, 77,
80, 81

surrogate, 4

surveyor, 4

tax on tea, 23, 24, 25, 26

Trespass Act, (1783), 61

U.S. Constitution, 76, 77, 78, 85

Washington, George, 41, 43, 56,
88, 119

Clinton, George (provincial governor),
1, 2

Clinton, James (brother), 55

Colden, Cadwallader, 3, 4, 12, 38

Committee for Detecting and
Defeating Conspiracies
(Tories), 61

Committee of Fifty-one (1774), 28

Committee of Sixty (1775), 36, 37, 38

H

Hamilton, Alexander, 67, 70, 73, 78,
79, 82, 84

Haring, John, 39

Henry, Patrick, 68

Hudson River Valley, 37, 46, 52

I

Impost, 64, 70, 71, 72, 73

Intolerable Acts (1775), 27, 28

J

Jauncey, 15, 25

Jay, John, 29, 47, 52, 53, 54, 56, 82

Jefferson, Thomas, 85, 88

K

Kaminski, John P., 102, 131

Kings College, 54

Kingston, 3, 28, 30, 53

Kissan, 25, 33

L

Lamb, John, 39

Lansing, Robert, 79

Lee, John K., 104, 131

Lee, Richard Henry, 47, 48, 68

Lewis, Francis, 39, 48

Lexington, Battle of, 40, 41

Little Britain, 1

Livingston faction, xii, 3, 4, 5, 7, 8, 9,
13, 14, 15, 16, 19, 20, 22, 24, 25,
26, 31, 36, 40, 54

Livingston, Peter R., 25

Livingston, Philip, 16, 29, 54

Livingston, Robert R., 25, 39

Livingston, William, 3, 8

Low, Isaac, 29, 39

Loyalists, 29, 30, 32, 38, 43, 46, 51, 61

M

Madison, James, 82

Mason, Bernard, 131

Mason, George, 68

McDougall, Alexander, 18, 19, 31, 39

McKesson, John, 43

Mechanics, 7, 27, 46, 47, 52

Methodists, 9, 12

Monroe, James, 68

Montesquieu, Baron de, 84

Montgomery, 55

Montreal, 3

Moore, Henry (Royal Governor),
13, 17

Morris, Lewis, 15, 16, 39

Mushkat, Jerome, 131

N

Newburgh, 2

New Windsor, 26, 28, 30

D r. Leo V. Kanawada Jr. was born in 1941 in Flushing, Long Island, New York, and educated at Bucknell University, where he received his Bachelor of Science Degree in Secondary Education. His Master of Arts Degree in American History was awarded by The Maxwell School of Citizenship and Public Affairs at Syracuse University, and his Ph.D. in History by St. John's University, Jamaica, New York.

After serving as a decorated captain of Infantry, United States Army, with the Second Infantry Division in 1966 in South Korea and in the Vietnam War in 1967 with the 71st Assault Helicopter Company and as a platoon leader with the 196th Light Infantry Brigade, Americal Division, Kanawada returned to his hometown and taught in the Hicksville Public Schools for thirty years. In the Department of History at Hicksville High School, he created and taught a Humanities Honors Program for the Gifted and Talented and was later honored and inducted into the Hicksville Hall of Fame.

He was also cited in *Who's Who in New York*, in *Who's Who Among America's Teachers*, and in *The Directory of American Scholars.*

His first book, authored in 1982, was a scholarly work on the presidency and American Foreign Policy entitled *Franklin D. Roosevelt's Diplomacy and American Catholics, Italians, and Jews* (UMI Research Press/Pro Quest). And later as an elder and president of his church, he published *Something Worthwhile: The Life and Times of The Parkway Community Church, 1629-1981* (Exposition Press). In 2011 after more than a decade of research, writing, and devotion, he completed the five volumes in *The Holocaust Diaries* (AuthorHouse), a novelized history series based on trustworthy historical evidence and credible research, documenting the extensive efforts of President Franklin D. Roosevelt and Pope Pius XII that saved millions of Jews in Nazi-controlled Europe during the Holocaust in World War Two. A real labor of love.

In one of his more recent books, his Vietnam War memoir entitled *Captain, Infantry* (AuthorHouse) –- which is a riveting and colorful account profusely illustrated by personal letters and a FACEBOOK page of almost 300 photos available for public use –- he provides a unique personal eyewitness panorama of his actions and activities as a U.S. Army ROTC infantry officer during his two-year, active-duty assignment in South Korea and in South Vietnam during the mid-1960s. And finally, in an inspirational account also profusely illustrated by several diaries and daily logs, a FACEBOOK page of 140 photos available for public use, personal letters and numerous newspaper articles, Kanawada's book, *The Jubilee Jamboree* (AuthorHouse), provides an eyewitness portrayal of the activities and travels of the 1,700 Boy Scouts in the American contingent along with the more than 35,000 scouts from 90 countries of the world to a once-in-a-lifetime World Jamboree gathering in the summer of 1957 in Sutton Park, England, celebrating the fiftieth anniversary of the birth of scouting and the one-hundredth anniversary of the birth of the founder of Boy Scouting, Sir Robert Baden-Powell. And Dr. Leo V. Kanawada Jr., at that time a fifteen-year-old Eagle Scout from the United States, was one of those young men.

Leo V. Kanawada Jr., lives with his wife, Carol, in Long Island, New York.

James Madison

In Memorium

We the People

"We the People of the United States, in Order to form a more perfect Union, establish Justice, insure domestic Tranquility, provide for the common defence, promote the general Welfare, and secure the Blessings of Liberty to ourselves and our Posterity, do ordain and establish this Constitution for the United States of America."

Preamble of the *Constitution of the United States of America*, 1787

9 781665 564755